D0828996

"To call this book 'a breath of fresh air' would be an understatement. This book is a gift from God. These women of God represent the power of God to break down the walls of separation, sexism, chauvinism, and misogyny in ministry. The breath of God breathes through every line and every sermon and demonstrates to the world how powerful and awesome our God really is. I celebrate their ministry. I praise God for their preaching, and I recommend this work to every African American church of every denomination."

REV. DR. JEREMIAH A. WRIGHT, JR., PASTOR EMERITUS
Trinity UCC, Chicago, Illinois

"Why volume two? Indeed, there is a Word from the Lord, and I believe it is important for us to hear the sacred text as interpreted by these sisters. The powerful homiletical voices of these sisters come from deep wells of hope, joy, and pain, with the realization that God is yet speaking. The sermons in this volume surely will challenge, soothe, and encourage the heart! Yes, emphatically, say it sisters!"

REV. DR. JUDY D. CUMMINGS, SENIOR PASTOR
New Covenant Christian Church (Disciples of Christ), Nashville, Tennessee

"This is a long-needed, most-welcome addition to our Womanist resources. This collection of sermons is well-anchored theologically and culturally. Each preacher has addressed the needs of the people, yet did not bow solely to their wants. Any pastor or preacher, regardless of gender or denominational affiliation, would be aided and well-served by these clear-minded voices of Black women preachers who have wrestled with biblical texts and have delivered blessings!"

REV. DR. DARRYL AARON, PASTOR
First Baptist Church , Winston-Salem, North Carolina

"These mighty Word warriors are not surrogates for the male or female gender; rather they are voices to be reckoned with and heard. They come in the Spirit with power; they are energized, sanctified, battle-scarred, and justified—what an awesome grouping. They have caught the spirit; they awaken us."

DR. RALPH T. GRANT, JR., VICE PRESIDENT OF OPERATIONS
Pillar College, Newark, New Jersey

THESE

Sisters

CAN *Say*

IT!

VOLUME 2

20 More Powerful Sermons from Contemporary
African American Women Preachers

To Glenesa

May you be blessed

& encouraged

by the Word!

THESE
Sisters
CAN *Say*
IT!

VOLUME 2

20 More Powerful Sermons from Contemporary
African American Women Preachers

EDITED BY
MARTHA SIMMONS & DARRYL D. SIMS

MMGI BOOKS · CHICAGO

THESE SISTERS CAN SAY IT! VOLUME 2
20 More Powerful Sermons from Contemporary African American Women Preachers

Copyright © 2014 by MMGI Books, Chicago, IL 60636

All rights reserved. Except for brief quotations used in reviews, articles, or other media, no part of this book may be reproduced or transmitted in any form or by any means, electronic or mechanical, including photocopying, recording, or by information storage or retrieval system, without permission of the publisher.

Except for quotations from Scripture, the quoted ideas expressed in the book are not in all cases exact quotations, as some have been edited for clarity and brevity. In all cases, the editors have attempted to maintain the speaker's original intent. In some cases, quoted material for this book was obtained from secondary sources, primarily print media. While every effort was made to ensure the accuracy of these sources, the accuracy cannot be guaranteed. For additions, deletions, corrections, or classifications in future editions of this text, please write Manuscript Management Group, Inc., P.O. Box 368163, Chicago, IL 60636.

Scriptures marked KJV are from the King James Version.

Scriptures marked The Message are from The Message, copyright © Eugene H. Peterson 1993, 1994, 1995. Used by permission of NavPress Publishing Group.

Scriptures marked NIV are from the Holy Bible, New International Version, copyright © 1973, 1978, 1984 by International Bible Society. Used by permission of Zondervan Publishing House. All rights reserved.

Scriptures marked NKJV are from the New King James Version, copyright © 1982 by Thomas Nelson, Inc. Used by permission. All rights reserved.

Scriptures marked NLT are from the Holy Bible, New Living Translation, copyright © 1996. Used by permission of Tyndale House Publishers , Inc. Wheaton, Illinois 60189. All rights reserved.

Scriptures marked NRSV are from the New Revised Standard Version Bible, copyright © 1989, Division of Christian Education of the National Council of the Churches of Christ in the United Stated of America. Used by permission. All rights reserved.

Library of Congress Cataloging-in-Publication Data

These Sisters Can Say It! 20 More Powerful Sermons from Contemporary African American Women Preachers

Edited by Martha Simmons and Darryl D. Sims

p. cm

ISBN 978-1-939774-07-1 (pbk. : alk. paper)

Black women – Religious life. 2. Black women – Conduct of life. 3. Black women – Development.

Printed in the U.S.A.

This book is dedicated to the tireless women who work arduously within our society and never receive the accolades due them; to the women who are devoted to speaking the loudest, by way of their actions, without uttering a single word; to the women who are faithful to their God, their family, and their communities; and to the women who will not give up on making this world a better place for all of God's children.

Contents

DISCIPLESHIP AND FAITH

Preface

Women have always had something to say on behalf of Christ. It was a woman who told the disciples that Jesus rose from the grave. It was women who were the first to proclaim, after Christ's burial and resurrection, that our Savior lives.

We are honored to present twenty sermons by a magnificent group of women preachers. *These Sisters can say it!* These talented preachers come from an array of backgrounds and denominations. They are anointed women of God. They are pastors, professors, entrepreneurs, evangelists, administrators, prophets, and scholars.

It was a goal of MMGI BOOKS to assemble a cadre of women preachers who truly represent our diverse faith community. We also wanted to include women whose preaching would reach a cross-section of society. After you read this book, we believe that you will say as we did, mission accomplished.

In this second volume of *These Sisters Can Say It!* we are introducing fresh voices, along with seasoned and well-known trumpeters of Calvary. As you read their sermons, you will sense from these preachers a passionate commitment to social justice, empowerment, discipleship, evangelism, faith, and identity formation. Excellent for retreats, conferences, Bible studies, and homiletic classes, these sermons offer much-needed life-changing information and inspiration. Indeed, *these sisters can say it!*

Acknowledgments

Martha and I applaud each preacher for her rich and thoughtful contributions to this book. We thank you for not being afraid to place in print the complex issues and deep passions that we as a society wrestle with on a daily basis. We also acknowledge the efforts of the entire MMGI team—Wendy, LaTanya, Victoria, Joanne, and Melodee. Without this team of professionals, MMGI would not be able to produce consistently high-quality books. Thank you.

Darryl D. Sims
Managing Partner
MMGI BOOKS

RESTORATION
AND JUSTICE

The Help

Eboni Marshall Turman

BIO. IN BRIEF
Reverend Eboni Marshall Turman, Ph.D.,
is Assistant Research Professor of Black Church Studies and
Director of the Office of Black Church Studies at The Divinity
School, Duke University. She is the youngest woman to
be licensed and ordained by the historic Abyssinian Baptist
Church in the City of New York, where she was the first woman
to serve as the Assistant Minister in Abyssinian's 205-year
history. Dr. Turman is the author of *Toward a Womanist
Ethic of Incarnation: Black Bodies, the Black Church, and
the Council of Chalcedon* (Palgrave Macmillan, 2013).

Psalm 51:1-10 (King James Version)
*Have mercy upon me, O God, according to thy loving kindness; according
unto the multitude of thy tender mercies blot out my transgressions.
Wash me thoroughly from mine iniquity and cleanse me from my sin.
For I acknowledge my transgressions, and my sin is ever before me.
Against thee, thee only, have I sinned and done this evil in thy sight;
that thou mightest be justified when thou speakest, and be clear when
thou judgest. Behold I was shapen in iniquity; and in sin did my mother*

conceive me. Behold thou desirest truth in the inward parts; and in the hidden part thou shalt make me to know wisdom. Purge me with hyssop, and I shall be clean; wash me and I shall be whiter than snow. Make me to hear joy and gladness, that the bones which thou hast broken may rejoice. Hide thy face from my sins and blot out all mine iniquities. Create in me a clean heart, O God; and renew a right spirit within me.

"Wash me thoroughly from mine iniquities and cleanse me from my sin. Create in me a clean heart, O God, and renew a right spirit within me." As I have reflected on the significance of washing, and cleansing, and purging in this morning's text, I am inspired to speak with you today on the subject: The Help.

Almost 75 years ago on February 29, 1940, one Hattie McDaniel, the daughter of former slaves, the youngest of thirteen children, a child of Wichita, Kansas, became the **first** African American, male or female, to win an Academy Award for her role as "the help" in the racially-charged 1939 motion picture "Gone with the Wind." And lest we romanticize this first in American history, one that disturbingly resurfaces in the pomp and circumstance of Octavia Spencer's 72-year-later Oscar win for her role as "the help" in 2012—lest we romanticize the exploitation and commodification of black women's labor with an image of a smiling fictitious Mammy, contrary to the imagination of white supremacy and its popular culture that would have us believe that we were shuckin' and jivin', Steppin and Fetchit people—we need to know that although over 75% of Black women worked as domestics at a point in our nation's history, our mothers and grandmothers, our great grandmothers and godmothers, our aunties and our sisters did not scrub white women's floors because they wanted to do it. They did not nurse white children because they wanted to. They did not withstand the sexual assault of white men because they wanted to.

Oh no, as Malcolm X so astutely observed, black women did not gather on the street corners of Harlem during the Great Depression, as white women drove by to bid on their domestic day labor—they did not gather there because they wanted to. No! They gathered in the slave markets of the Bronx and Upper Manhattan because they had to—because they had children to feed and they had brothers and sisters to put through school, because they had communities to invest in, dreams to build, and churches to support.

Delores S. Williams, a mother of womanist theology, would call this voluntary surrogacy, but I'll keep it simple and say that you wouldn't have what you have right now—the shoes on your feet, the clothes on your back, the food in your belly, the prayer in your quiver, the scripture on your tongue, the song in your heart—you would not have what you have right now if it hadn't been for Big Momma, if it hadn't been for Nana, if it hadn't been for Ma Dear doing what they did not want to do so that you would have a chance to do more than you could have ever imagined.

And this is exactly where we find God in our text this morning. In the 51st Psalm, we are introduced to a God who amidst unseemly circumstances is called upon to clean and to wash, a God who is called upon to blot out and to renew; in other words, we find a God who in the very yearnings of the psalmist is identified as "The help." Well, someone might say, Reverend, that's blasphemous, how can you say that God is "The help"? How can you dare contend, Black woman, that God's identity corresponds with the substance of Black women's reality; that is, that according to womanist theological matriarch Jacquelyn Grant, God is *homoousious* with Black women as to their humanity?

Well, I didn't write the Bible; I am just telling you what it says, and in the seventh chapter of 1 Samuel when Israel subdued the Philistines, Samuel placed a rock between Mizpeh and Shen and called its name Ebenezer, saying, the Lord *helped* us. In the 46th division of the Psalter, it is written, "God is our refuge and our strength, a very present *help* in times of trouble." I stopped by the sanctuary of God this morning to tell somebody about a God who is our help in ages past, our hope for years to come, a shelter from the stormy blast and our eternal home. God is our help!

Now, don't get it twisted—just because God is our help does not mean that God always wants to help us. You see, some scholars suggest that the 51st Psalm corresponds with David's rape of Bathsheba and the murder of her husband, Uriah. Here, then, we find David the rapist and David the murderer calling upon the mercies of God. Some may be uncomfortable with my calling it like it is; nevertheless, however, as we come to interpret this scripture, one thing is clear—the writer is in deep trouble. Something has gone terribly wrong—for the first thing we find the psalmist saying is, "Have mercy on me, O LORD, according to thy loving kindness." He says, "Blot out my transgressions according to thy tender mercies." I acknowledge my transgressions, but, as Teresa Fry Brown would say, "Can a sista get a little help?" "My sin is ever before me," but can a brother get a little help?

You can play bad if you want to, but I know that someone in here today has been in trouble before. In fact somebody is in trouble right now—and you're thinking, "Help! I've got to go to the doctor this week for some tests. Help! My husband, my wife is being deployed. Help! I went to work last week and got laid off. Help! I'm pregnant and I don't know what to do. Help! I've got to fight a charge in court tomorrow. Help! I am about to be evicted, kicked out onto the street." That's right, somebody is in trouble right now. Turn to your neighbor and say, "Help!"

That's right, somebody is in trouble! And you know how I know? Let me say it this way. When I was a little girl my mother would make me clean my room, and I never wanted to clean my room because it was so messy that it would take all day. So I would go into my room and shove all of my toys and all of my things under the bed quickly! I would ball up my clothes with one hand and toss them into the closet out of my mother's line of vision. And when she would come in to inspect my room, the surface would sparkle and no junk was immediately visible. But as soon as my mother would open the closet door my façade would be shattered; as soon as she looked under the bed, all my mess would be revealed. You may look good on the outside this morning, as Drake says, "Hair done, nails done, everything did." You may be sparkling on the surface, but your inner closet tells a different story. You've got some mess up under your bed, and some of you left some mess in your bed this morning, but that's another sermon. Everything that glitters ain't gold, and no matter how good we look on the surface, we all have or have had trouble in our lives.

Some of us have spiritual trouble. We cannot bring ourselves to pray, though we have heard it said, "Cast all your cares upon him for he careth for you."[1] Some of us have health trouble and we think it is the end, so we won't even bother going to the doctor, though the Word of God tells us that "by His stripes we are healed."[2] Some of us have emotional trouble;

we are bereaved. We can't get over Mama dying, or our spouse transitioning, though we have heard it said there is no more dying over there, there is no more crying there, that every day is like Sunday. Some of us are facing financial trouble, though we have heard it said, "Give and it shall be given unto you, good measure, pressed down, shaken together and running over…"[3] Some of us have relationship trouble (Cheryl Townsend Gilkes said it best, we are "in love and in trouble"[4]) but we won't get rid of that sorry so and so because we are afraid of being alone, although we have heard it said, "Lo, I will be with you always even until the end of the age."[5]

Some of us have serious trouble of our own making, and according to the justice of God, we don't deserve God's help. In fact, the psalmist says in our text, "I have done evil in your sight and you are justified to judge me." Sometimes our transgressions are not about our love lives, or our financial realities, or health challenges—no, sometimes our transgressions really are so depraved that God should not help us. Maybe you are not a racist, but you are bound by colorist pygmatocracy—you prefer your friends to be lighter than a paper bag. Maybe you are not colorist, but you are sexist, always preferring men's leadership to women's. Maybe you are not sexist, but you are classist, always with your nose stuck up in the air, treating other folk as if they are less than you are. Maybe you are not classist, but you are heterosexist,[6] quick to point out the speck in your neighbor's eye without taking account of the log in your own. Sometimes our lives are so pitiful that God would be justified in not helping us, in judging us as we are—as the lying and thieving, conniving, and petty people that we are. But I'm so glad that though I am not what I should be, it does not yet appear what I shall become—and because of that "amazing grace that saved a wretch like me," and because of God's great faithfulness, "Great is thy faithfulness, O God my father, there is no shadow of turning in thee; thou changest not, thy compassions they fail not, as thou hast been thy forever will be."[7] Because of God's loving kindness, because of God's tender mercies, I am so glad that God is compelled by the wretched condition of his children and his love for us, to go out and clean up our dirty houses on our behalf even when he really shouldn't. Oh yes, we have got some houses in need of cleaning, which is why the psalmist says, "Wash me thoroughly from mine iniquity and cleanse me from my sin." Our earthly houses have been defiled by the trickery of the evil one and only the help of God can clean things up.

For him, the psalmist says, "Lord, it is so bad that even my bones have been broken, but I know that you have the power to make even that which thou hast broken rejoice." So in spite of everything else, Lord, just give me a clean heart and renew a right spirit within me. In other words, the psalmist is saying, Lord, help me right now—I need something to change drastically in my life right now. I need something to shift in my spirit, right now.

Now, you cannot get a clean heart just by asking for it. No. In order to get a clean heart and a "new spirit" you have to be willing to get rid of your defiled heart and the funky spirit that you have right now. In the ancient world, the heart was not a reference for the emotional center of personality. The heart actually signified the mind and the will, so that a reference to a clean heart actually means that one desires a transformed mind, a new way of thinking. There are too many of us trying to lay claim to a "new" spirit when the truth is that we are still carrying that spirit of bitterness about something that happened

10 years ago. We are claiming a new spirit when our lips are still stuck out about something that happened last week. We are claiming a new spirit and are still ticked off by a dream that God didn't bring to fruition. If you want a new spirit, you are going to have to get rid of the ungodly spirit that's on you right now. You may have a spirit of fear, or maybe you have a spirit of deception. Maybe you have a gossiping spirit, maybe you have a depressed spirit, or maybe you're just mean-spirited. Whatever your case is today, somebody needs to know that you've got HELP.

Jesus says, when you pray, pray in this way, saying, "Abba, Father," but I am here to tell you that like a *good mother* **and** a *good father*, God will do whatever it takes to help God's children. And no matter how dirty you are feeling this morning, no matter how filthy your house may be, God has a special cleansing formula that was designed with you in mind. No, I am not talking about Clorox, Comet, or Mr. Clean. I'm not talking about Fantastic, Febreze, or 409. God has his own cleaning formula! It's one part living water (Jesus said, "I am the living water that never runs dry, he who drinks of the water I give shall never thirst"[8]), and it's one part oil ("Thou anointest my head with oil; my cup runneth over"[9]). It's one part living water and one part oil of the Spirit, but the formula would not be complete without its most potent ingredient. My grandmother knew all about it, because on every first Sunday she would wake up singing, "There is a fountain, filled with blood drawn from Immanuel's veins, and sinners plunged beneath that flood, lose all their guilty stains. The dying thief rejoiced to see that fountain in his day. And there may I, though vile as he, wash all my sins away."[10] It's nothing but the blood of Jesus!

Well, someone is thinking, My house is so dirty that God will have to wash me over and over again, and everybody knows that if you keep washing the same thing over and over again, eventually it will get dingy and worn out. Well, the good news is that God has already prepared an exigency plan. You see, Paul said, that "when this earthly tabernacle be dissolved" (when it gets dingy and worn out, the elders say, "There's a leak in this old building and my soul has got to move"), when this old earthly tabernacle is dissolved, Paul says, "We have a building of God, an house not made with hands, eternal in the heavens."[11] Jesus said, "Let not your heart be troubled. Ye believe in God, believe also in me. In my Father's house are many mansions…"[12] All I'm trying to tell you is that we've got just The (capital T) Help we need!

And since Black women have been cast in the wrong role for centuries now, I stopped by on this first Sunday in Women's Month to make a new nomination. Our Savior has never walked a red carpet, but he did walk up Golgotha's hill. Our God has never held an Oscar, but he holds the whole world in his hand. He's not Denzel or Tom Hanks, because he's not an actor; he's just the star of the greatest story ever told. So if you need some **help** this morning, or when you go to the office tomorrow, or when you are trying to find a job this week, or if you're dodging Peter to pay Paul, don't look at me because I need **The Help** too. Look to Jesus, for he is our refuge and our strength, a very present **help** in times of trouble. My grandmother says he's a way maker, a bridge over troubled water, a bright and morning star, a heart fixer and a mind regulator! So I will lift up mine eyes to the hills from whence cometh my **help**; my **help** comes from the Lord, the maker of heaven and earth, the ruler and super-ruler of the universe.

NOTES

1. 1 Peter 5:7, KJV.

2. Isaiah 53:5, KJV.

3. Luke 6:38a, KJV.

4. Cheryl Townsend Gilkes, "The Loves and 'Troubles' of African American Women's Bodies," in *A Troubling in My Soul: Womanist Perspectives on Evil and Suffering*, ed. Emilie M. Townes (Maryknoll, NY: Orbis Books, 1993), 232–50.

5. Matthew 28:20, KJV.

6. According to Wikipedia (http://en.wikipedia.org/wiki/Heterosexism), heterosexism is a system of attitudes, bias, and discrimination in favor of opposite-sex sexuality and relationships. It can include the presumption that other people are heterosexual or that opposite-sex attractions and relationships are the only norm and therefore superior. Although heterosexism is defined in the online editions of the *American Heritage Dictionary of the English Language* and the *Merriam-Webster Collegiate Dictionary* as anti-gay discrimination and/or prejudice "by heterosexual people" and "by heterosexuals," respectively, people of any sexual orientation can hold such attitudes and bias. Nonetheless, heterosexism as discrimination ranks gays, lesbians, bisexuals and other sexual minorities as second-class citizens with regard to various legal and civil rights, economic opportunities, and social equality in many of the world's jurisdictions and societies. Heterosexism is often related to homophobia.

7. Thomas O. Chisholm, "Great Is Thy Faithfulness." *African American Heritage Hymnal* (Chicago, IL: GIA Press, 2001), #158.

8. John 4:14b, paraphrased.

9. Psalm 23:5b, KJV.

10. William Cowper, "There Is a Fountain." *African American Heritage Hymnal* (Chicago, IL: GIA Press, 2001), #257.

11. 2 Corinthians 5:1b, KJV.

12. John 14:1-2a, KJV.

Restoring the Dance of Our Daughters

Neichelle Guidry Jones

BIO. IN BRIEF

Reverend Neichelle Guidry Jones is a spiritual daughter of New Creation Christian Fellowship of San Antonio, Texas. She is a graduate of Clark Atlanta University (BA, Lambda Pi Eta) and Yale Divinity School (M.Div.), where she was the 2010 recipient of the Walcott Prize for Clear and Effective Public and Pulpit Speaking. Neichelle is a Doctor of Philosophy student in Liturgical Studies at Garrett-Evangelical Theological Seminary in Evanston, Illinois. She is also the Associate Pastor to Young Adults at Trinity United Church of Christ in Chicago.

Judges 11:1-10, 29-40 (New Revised Standard Version)

Now Jephthah the Gileadite, the son of a prostitute, was a mighty warrior. Gilead was the father of Jephthah. Gilead's wife also bore him sons; and when his wife's sons grew up, they drove Jephthah away, saying to him, "You shall not inherit anything in our father's house; for you are the son of another woman." Then Jephthah fled from his brothers and lived in the land of Tob. Outlaws collected around Jephthah and went raiding with him.

After a time the Ammonites made war against Israel. And when the Ammonites made war against Israel, the elders of Gilead went to bring Jephthah from the land of Tob. They said to Jephthah, "Come and be our commander, so that we may fight with the Ammonites." But Jephthah said to the elders of Gilead, "Are you not the very ones who rejected me and drove me out of my father's house? So why do you come to me now when you are in trouble?" The elders of Gilead said to Jephthah, "Nevertheless, we have now turned back to you, so that you may go with us and fight with the Ammonites, and become head over us, over all the inhabitants of Gilead." Jephthah said to the elders of Gilead, "If you bring me home again to fight with the Ammonites, and the Lord gives them over to me, I will be your head." And the elders of Gilead said to Jephthah, "The LORD will be witness between us; we will surely do as you say."

Then the spirit of the LORD came upon Jephthah, and he passed through Gilead and Manasseh. He passed on to Mizpah of Gilead, and from Mizpah of Gilead he passed on to the Ammonites. And Jephthah made a vow to the LORD, and said, "If you will give the Ammonites into my hand, then whoever comes out of the doors of my house to meet me, when I return victorious from the Ammonites, shall be the LORD's, to be offered up by me as a burnt offering." So Jephthah crossed over to the Ammonites to fight against them; and the LORD gave them into his hand. He inflicted a massive defeat on them from Aroer to the neighborhood of Minnith, twenty towns, and as far as Abel-keramim. So the Ammonites were subdued before the people of Israel. Then Jephthah came to his home at Mizpah; and there was his daughter coming out to meet him with timbrels and with dancing. She was his only child; he had no son or daughter except her. When he saw her, he tore his clothes, and said, "Alas, my daughter! You have brought me very low; you have become the cause of great trouble to me. For I have opened my mouth to the LORD, and I cannot take back my vow." She said to him, "My father, if you have opened your mouth to the LORD, *do to me according to what has gone out of your mouth, now that the* LORD *has given you vengeance against your enemies, the Ammonites." And she said to her father, "Let this thing be done for me: Grant me two months, so that I may go and wander on the mountains, and bewail my virginity, my companions and I." "Go," he said and sent her away for two months. So she departed, she and her companions, and bewailed her virginity on the mountains. At the end of two months, she returned to her father, who did with her according to the vow he had made. She had never slept with a man. So there arose an Israelite custom that for four days every year the daughters of Israel would go out to lament the daughter of Jephthah the Gileadite.*

In 1971, Alvin Ailey debuted a dance entitled "Cry." The dance was a gift to his mother, and it was dedicated to Black women, "especially Black mothers," everywhere. In its debut, Judith Jamison, who would go on to become the Artistic Director of the Alvin Ailey American Dance Theater, performed the dance and secured its place in the American artistic imagination. "Cry" is a 16-minute solo, composed of three parts wherein the dancer illustrates a trajectory that is common in the lives of many Black women. Over the three parts, we see the woman wrestle with bondage and spin and leap her way into liberation. When asked about the experience, Jamison responded, "One of the hardest things to do is to finish it without looking exhausted."

Similarly, many of us go through such chapters in our lives. From bondage to liberation, and then from bondage to liberation all over again. And we know that it is often very difficult to arise from a fight, to emerge from a season of fighting, without feeling exhausted and depleted, simply from the events themselves. Not to mention the residual, the leftovers, the aftermath, the baggage that results from the battles. And as I've thought about these realities within the wider context of our lives, I've come up with just a few questions: How does one dance with all the baggage that she has accumulated and that she carries on a daily basis? How does one go through life with all of its contents, with all of its weight bearing down on our spirits, our bodies? And finally, I ask, how can we release the weight and restore the dance, and how can the sacrificed life of a little nameless daughter of antiquity speak to these questions?

And so, before we begin speaking of this daughter in the text, let me see where the daughters are in the room. It doesn't matter how old or young you are. If you are a woman in here today, you are somebody's daughter.

You, who descend from your kinfolk, with your kinfolk's name, some similar countenances, and perhaps even some inherited issues; you, who found yourself, young and female, born into a familial system with your lives coded with cultural mores, you found yourself beginning to piece together your identity by virtue of the relationships you shared with those you came to know as family.

Where are you, daughters?

I could be ruffling someone's feathers with this, because I know that being a daughter is often a very complex thing. I know that by bringing up the fact that we are all someone's daughters that I am conjuring images and memories of your family:

- Your siblings, your blood siblings, and your sisters from other misters and bothers from other mothers
- Your mama, your daddy—whether they were around or whether their roles were fulfilled by someone else

- Your aunties and uncles
- Your grandmothers and grandfathers
- The ones who raised you and even the ones you raised. I may even be reminding you of the way that you raised yourself and perhaps a few others. And now today, you only identify yourself as a daughter of God—if that.
- People and moments (joys, juggling, and triumphs)

I know that being a daughter can be complex. Even in the most ideal of daughter-to-family relationships, daughters are often charged with the all-too-dismaying task of figuring out what it means to be a good daughter inside of her family: One who is responsible and makes sound decisions, even if it costs her her own dreams and identity. One who is selfless, and always thinks about her family first. One who is diligent, following the plans that have been laid out before her or improvising creatively where there is no plan at all. You are someone's daughter. We are someone's daughters.

And we are not alone in the room. Meet another one of us, another daughter. She can be found down deep in the annals of the Hebrew Scriptures and in the pew right next to you, alongside her family and her friends. Meet the girl, bright with a mind of deep thought and acute perception, lit by the light of her dreams and hopes, called apart for her potential and promise. The girl with the skill of warming hearts, because joy like hers is rare and hope like the kind she possesses is hard to come by.

She has a heart unfettered by distrust. A body, always ready to break out in a dance.

A spirit, enlivened by the very Spirit of God.

She has a dance about her,
It seems as if music follows her.
She is always seeking to celebrate someone, like a father
home from battle.

She is eager to love,
Eager to be loved,
Hungry for acceptance and thirsty for affirmation,
Always looking for joy.

She is looking for you
To see her,
To pay attention to her,
To look beyond her budding breasts and her widening
hips and her round derrière.
She is more than a body, more than hair and nails.
She is a mind. A spirit. A soul. A child of God.

And yet, this girl is often looked over. She is often looked
over in favor of the brothers and the sons. She is often
misguided by images of flawless bodies and reckless love, until
she's become lost on a search for *some kind of validation*.

She is often forced to carry more responsibility than her
young back can hold up, and before she knows it, the young
girl is fighting for her dreams, fighting for her divine identity,
fighting for her life. And in the fight for her life, she learns to do
what it takes to survive. And when surviving takes precedence
over thriving—when it becomes more important that a young
woman *merely makes it* and stops *deeply living*, she becomes
intimately familiar with isolation, low self-esteem, and poor
self-image. She loses her imagination, hope, self-sense, and
maybe even her life—**she loses her dance!**

I believe that this girl's story has some answers to the questions we are asking this morning. But, first, I need to get into the crevices of her background a little bit. Because her background provides the context, the backdrop, for her life.

Yes, she is caught in the matrix of her own issues, but her family history is such that it almost predisposes her to all of them. In other words, this girl was **born into baggage**. She almost has no say in some of the issues she navigates, as she's got bags that she has no name for, because she had nothing to do with their presence in her life.

She did not pack these bags. This daughter was born into baggage.

Anyone know what it means to be born into baggage? It means that you were thrust from the peace of your mother's womb into the complexities of this human experience. It means that you were born to imperfect people and imperfect families and communities, all of whom knew nothing about what to do with their issues, how to release their baggage.

This is just like the daughter in our text. Meet her father, Jephthah. Mighty judge. Valiant warrior. A man with his own bags that he never laid down. He's got family issues. He was an "invalid" son because his mother was a woman of the night. He was a rejected brother who got no share of his father's inheritance or his family's love. He has a destructive kind of piety.

See, he was an unfathered *boy*—who never had the influence of a father, never had anyone to hand the traditions down to him, and to teach him the ways of his people and his God. Never had someone to tell him that in the case of Abraham, God provided a ram in a bush to keep him from sacrificing his son. No one told him that sending children through fire was not always pleasing to God. And for a warrior whose concept of family was synonymous with rejection, who never knew love, and who was never properly mothered *or* fathered, I find it difficult that he could conceive of a God who could be pleased without some act of **physical or emotional** violence.

So not only was she born into her father's baggage, but she was also born into the baggage of her larger context. She was born and raised in a place where death was more favorable than bringing dishonor to her father. Why, her father was **Jephthah, the Judge**. He had just conquered the Ammonites and was finally about to be reunited with his family—on his terms. He was about to ascend to prominence and power since he had proven himself in battle. What would happen to him if *she* stood between him and his God, his world, and his image as a mighty warrior and a strong man at this critical time?

Furthermore, where was her mother? Where was *a* mother? Someone to tell her about the special way that God related to God's daughters? A keeper of the wisdom of the women—someone to tell her that just a few judges ago, a woman reigned from a palm tree and another woman went to battle for her people and was victorious? Someone to tell her that women were not necessarily created to be in the background and to uphold a man's image just so he can feel "macho" or project a "macho" image?

And so not only was she born into the baggage of her family, the baggage of her context, but she was born into the baggage of crucial absences. The daughter had bags before she was born. Bags imposed on her. Bags all around her. So many of her problems were related to her status as a daughter.

I wish I had the time to get into the story and the intelligence to understand it and the answers as to WHY God let this happen to this girl. And the truth is that I know that a lot of us in here—sons and daughters—have lived with that very question: *God, why did you let this happen to me?* Whatever *this* is. We've wondered why God didn't intervene for us the way God did for somebody else. It just wasn't, or *isn't*, fair. *I didn't choose these bags!*

As this text and our lives boldly profess, God's ways are not always fair in our minds. God doesn't deal with us in terms of fairness. But what God does do is give us the strength to keep going on and the power to drop our bags—to keep dancing— until those answers come. And although her dance and her life were taken, in chapter 11 of Judges, this daughter's life gives us some suggestions for restoring our dances in the final verses of chapter 11.

First, she came out dancing. When I was growing up, I remember that around every major holiday our art projects in grade school would consist of handmade greeting cards and gifts to give to our parents. Mother's Day and Father's Day, Christmas, Thanksgiving, Easter. It seemed as if very early on, our teachers wanted to show us that there is an intrinsic value to what we could create as children. We didn't have any money, but there was something that we could give to express our creativity and our love. Throughout my life, this is something that I've struggled to maintain because I've become inundated in what I now know to call capitalism. Even with the memories of how those greeting cards would adorn Mom and Dad's offices and refrigerators, I still struggle to put in the time and the energy and the thought and intentionality into *creating* something *authentic* instead of going out and spending my money on mass-produced gifts.

This is why I love that this daughter chose to bless her father with a dance. It was an act of expression and joy, a display of her unfettered love and excitement that Dad was home, victorious in battle. She didn't know just how much was riding on this dance, but she came out of the house—dancing. Did she receive the word that the Lord had given her father victory over his enemies? Or was she just so excited to hear her father returning home, to learn that the Lord had spared his life in battle, to see him with her own two eyes? I can imagine her young feet prancing as her hands held the tambourine, dancing just because her dad was coming home. Dancing because that's what she did. If she were a runner, maybe she would have run to see him. If she were more of an analytic than an artist, perhaps she would have walked to meet him. But, in her creative genius and her artistic impulses, she came playing the tambourine and dancing to meet her father.

And in the course of her dance, she is met with her wailing father and the news that she has received a death sentence. Can you imagine this girl, dancing to the beat of her own drum, when all of a sudden her beat and her dance are stalled, and her life is stolen? How many times have the creativity and artistry, the eccentricity and the expression of our daughters been squelched because their families didn't understand them, or accept them? How many dreams have died because a child was told to forsake the dream and chase the check? How many gifts and talents have been thrown away because no one clapped for her or cheered for her?

How many beautiful heads have hung down low because she was never told that she was beautiful? How many of our daughters' voices have been silenced because she was ignored for too long, or told to quiet down? How many of her possibilities have been foreclosed because she wasn't affirmed, and wasn't strong enough to affirm herself? How many of our daughters have lost their dances? How many of our daughters' dances have been replaced with weeping and roaming, or even dying?

And in a culture that has convinced our youth that they live with their lives on the line, it seems hopeless that the dance can ever be recovered. She came out dancing, and her dance suggests that restoration of the dance begins with a re-embrace of that which is authentically you. This daughter prompts us to ask ourselves, *What gives me life, and gives life to my bones? What makes me want to dance? What comes so naturally to me that I couldn't shut it up or stop it, even if I tried?* As Howard Thurman said, "Don't ask what the world needs. Rather ask— what makes you come alive? Then go and do it! Because what the world needs is people who have come alive."[1]

Second, she received and conceded to her father's fatal decision, but not without some negotiation. In other words, although a girl, she spoke up. "You will have to do what you've promised, but not before I get two months to mourn." How many of us have resigned ourselves to carry this weight, this baggage without negotiating how much we can really handle? Without raising questions and gaining clarity? How many of us of have exercised some boldness and asked for what we need? One of the most tragic consequences of baggage is that it convinces us that we are not worthy of anything better. We get used to carrying it. We get used to its weight and its pressure, so much so that it becomes a part of who we are. And we don't stop and ask ANYONE for what we need and what we deserve!

When was the last time you asked somebody for *help* because you simply needed some help? Or called a licensed therapist because you *needed* to clear your head before crazy set in? Or asked the boss for a raise because you needed some more money to support you and your babies? Or asked your husband for a greater degree of intimacy because you needed it? Or asked your best girlfriend to get on a plane or get in her car or whatever, because you needed some girlfriend time to bring you back to center?

Do you know how to ask for something life-giving? For something that is good for you? Do you know how to ask for what you need? Woman, do you know how to speak up for yourself? Better yet—do you know how to show up for yourself? Do you know how to advocate for yourself? To do something to help yourself? To *obnoxiously impose* upon in order to ensure your own sanity? Like the woman at Bethany, and the woman with the flowing blood, who *spoke up for themselves*?

Or have you resigned yourself to living with dead weight? Have you resigned yourself to silence and acquiescence to this heavy lot in life? Do you know how to stand on the picket line with your sign, on strike until your own needs are met? Or do you not believe that your needs are important enough? Or do you not value your own humanity, or know the sound of your own voice?

Let me remind you that *you*, woman of faith, daughter of God, come from a line of women who knew what it meant to negotiate with God. And you have been invited to negotiate. You've been invited to represent yourself. To speak up for yourself and to act on your own behalf. *Ask and it's yours, seek and you'll find, knock and the door will be opened to you.*[2] If you want to restore your dance, you will need to speak up for yourself. Ask for what you need!

Finally, she went to the hills. A remote place. A hidden place. To mourn what would never be. She didn't go to mourn her death. She went to mourn what she would never experience. What happened up there? The text says that she wept with her friends.

Grieving is the ache that results from some detrimental loss—in the privacy of our hearts. It is the process by which our souls go through the valleys of life. Mourning, on the other hand, is what happens when that ache is made public. It is the wail, the shout, and the releasing of the tears. It is the disclosure and the representation of our pain. What made it public is that she didn't go up all by herself. She went up there with her girlfriends. She didn't go through this alone. She took some of her sisters with her.

Now, there's one kind of friend who will kick it when the kickin' is easy. But at the sign of difficulty, she's nowhere to be found. And then there's a girlfriend who will be *with* you when things get thick. The girlfriend who can handle your hills. And I believe that there are some of us here that would say that a girlfriend—a God-sent girlfriend—can mean the difference between life and death, surviving and thriving, and giving up and getting up.

And, so this daughter takes to the hills to let it be known that she was hurting. However, rather than living on with that hurt—that baggage—and taking it with her to her grave, the hills became a site of release and sharing. So there is good news here! Perhaps you've lost your dance because you were dancing a solo. The solo just seemed easier. With a solo, you don't have to wait on somebody else to rehearse. But somebody knows that a solo is more difficult. You have to carry the performance all by yourself.

Somebody knows that sometimes a duet or a company can make the load a little lighter. It may take a little more work. But, the restoration of the dance must often involve some other people, perhaps even some girlfriends. Ecclesiastes 4:13 says, "One can be overpowered, but two can defend themselves. And three is even better because a cord of 3 strands is not easily broken." Girl, you've got to be able to admit when you can't get your dance back by yourself. You need some girlfriends.

You need someone who can bear witness to the power of God, who reminds you of the God you serve and the promises God has made to keep you. A *girlfriend* who can remind you, *You've been through this before. God has fixed this before.* And one who will bear witness to what she sees in you, and will tell you, *You can do this! You can beat this. You can win this!*

And I'm so glad that we don't have to look to the hills to mourn anymore. But we can look to the hills from which cometh **our** help. Our help comes from the Lord. David said, "I will lift up mine eyes to the hills from which cometh my Help. My help cometh from the LORD, The LORD who made Heaven and earth. God will not suffer my foot to be moved"[3] because God is *my help*!

And when I hear the words of David, I begin to hear the voice of Jesus saying, "And I will ask the Father, and the Father will send you a HELPER":

- An Advocate when you don't have one.
- A friend when you don't have one.
- A voice when you don't have one.
- The Spirit of Truth who will cause you to remember and re-embrace the dance that God gave you.

- The Spirit who will give you boldness to speak up and show up for yourself.
- The Spirit who will draw you to the hills to mourn, to release, and to share.

The good news is that there are those young women who may have lost their dance at one point, but lived on to get it back, because of the Spirit of God.

There are those women who may have lost the beat and the rhythm of the music, but hung in there to hear it again. Because of the Spirit.

And so in the woman who decides that she is ready to resume her *dance*, this young girl lives on.

She says, dance, dance, dance; show off all of your moves.

Do it because of the Spirit who beckons us to be restored, and the same Spirit restores us, so that we all can dance, dance, dance!

NOTES

1. See Gil Bailie, *Violence Unveiled: Humanity at the Crossroads* (New York, NY: The Crossroad Publishing Company, 1996), xv, where he attributes the quotation to a conversation he had with Thurman.

2. Matthew 7:7, paraphrased.

3. Psalm 121, paraphrased.

Go to the Rock

Regina Henderson

BIO. IN BRIEF

Reverend Regina Henderson is an ordained elder in the North Carolina Conference of The United Methodist Church. She is a graduate of Howard University and Duke Divinity School. She currently serves as associate general secretary for Justice and Relationships at the General Board of Global Ministries of The United Methodist Church, which is located in New York City.

Exodus 17:1-7 (New International Version)

The whole Israelite community set out from the Desert of Sin, traveling from place to place as the LORD commanded. They camped at Rephidim, but there was no water for the people to drink. So they quarreled with Moses and said, "Give us water to drink." Moses replied, "Why do you quarrel with me? Why do you put the LORD to the test?"

But the people were thirsty for water there, and they grumbled against Moses. They said, "Why did you bring us up out of Egypt to make us and our children and livestock die of thirst?"

Then Moses cried out to the LORD, "What am I to do with these people? They are almost ready to stone me."

The LORD answered Moses, "Go out in front of the people. Take with you some of the elders of Israel and take in your hand the staff with which you struck the Nile, and go. I will stand there before you by the rock at Horeb. Strike the rock, and water will come out of it for the people to drink." So Moses did this in the sight of the elders of Israel. And he called the place Massah and Meribah because the Israelites quarreled and because they tested the LORD saying, "Is the LORD among us or not?"

Robert McCullough, John Gaines, Thomas Gaither, Clarence Graham, W.T. "Dub" Massey, Willie McLeod, James Wells, David Williamson, Jr., and Mack Workman. These are the names of the nine men who have come to be known as the Friendship 9. These are nine black college students who attended Friendship Junior College in Rock Hill, South Carolina. They found themselves in the upstream battle of racial and social injustice in the1960s and they were ready to swim for their lives and for justice for all. These brothers gained nationwide attention because they followed an untried strategy of "Jail, No Bail." This lessened the enormous financial burden civil rights groups were facing as the sit-in movement spread across the South.

The Friendship 9 sat in the section of a diner reserved for WHITES ONLY and engaged in a nonviolent protest. Had they raised their fists and fought with those who didn't want them seated, they may have been justified in doing so, but no good would have come of that. They would have been arrested for violence and they could not have prevailed in a southern court against such charges if they physically fought back.

So there they sat at the racially segregated McCrory's lunch counter during a crucial time in American history. It was a time when their state representative, Strom Thurman, known as one of the most ultra-conservative and racist politicians in US history, sat in the US Senate. They sat at that counter at a time when a fairly young Jesse Helms sat in as a nightly radio commentator lobbying hard against social justice and racial equality. The Friendship 9 sat refusing to get up eight years after the Montgomery Bus Boycott and shortly after the Greensboro Woolworth sit-in.

There the Friendship 9 sat long after the brutal beating of 14-year-old Emmett Till in Mississippi and long before the national reverberation of Martin King's "I Have a Dream" speech in Washington. There they sat at that York County lunch counter long after Brown v. Board of Education and long before Barbara Jordan entered the Texas Senate. There they sat disrupting the evils of injustice of the *old* Dirty South long after the Little Rock 9 in Arkansas and long before Congresswoman Shirley Chisholm launched her "Unbought and Unbossed" campaign in her quest to be the first black president.

There they sat making history shortly after Thurgood Marshall first sat at a Howard University law school desk and before Malcolm's murder. They sat long before "Bloody Sunday" in Montgomery, long before the formation of the Black Panthers, long before Stokely Carmichael coined the phrase "Black Power," and long before Dr. King's assassination in Memphis. They sat there while our denomination, now known as The *United* Methodist Church, was racially divided through what was known as the Central Jurisdiction. Long before Barack Obama stepped foot onto the White House lawn, there in Rock Hill, South Carolina, sat nine black college students taking a stand for justice by taking a seat!

Why bring up the Friendship 9? Some of you are likely asking, *Why go back in history? Why from the pulpit? And, Lord, why this Sunday? It's not Black History Month. Couldn't you have saved this message for the MLK holiday? Preacher, could not you have just chosen a lighter subject matter? Can't we just say a fervent prayer for all the oppressed, pass the collection plate for the poor, and move on? And, excuse me, Reverend, don't you know that I came to church to be inspired? Preacher, you are not going to make us sing, "We Shall Overcome," are you?!*

Well, let me just say for all of you out there who have already arrived. Who have already overcome. Who have p-u-l-l-e-d yourself up by your own bootstraps. Who have made all the right connections on your own. Rubbed shoulders with the right folk on your own. For those of you who have already moved on up to the East Side with George and Weezie. For all of you out there who have friends whose *fish don't fry in the kitchen* and whose *beans don't burn on the grill*, for all of you who think not talking about problems mean they don't exist, you are confused if you believe justice has arrived for all of us in these yet to be United States. I think the death of Trayvon Martin has reminded many of us that our fight for justice is ongoing and requires vigilant spirits, requires that we continue to stand up, and speak out.

Today I stand before you as I do every Sunday—not as a politician but as a pulpiteer. I stand before you today as I do every Sunday to proclaim the Good News of Jesus Christ. I do so as I do every Sunday through Scripture, my reasoning and understanding, the traditions of the Church, and through the lenses of my spiritual experience with God—specifically through the lenses of my spiritual experiences as a Black woman living in the United States of America.

And as *you* hear the Word proclaimed and come forth, you, in turn, interpret and receive that Word through the lenses of your own experiences as a child or as a youth or as a new believer or as a well-versed biblical scholar. You understand, then, that we cannot look at the teachings and preaching of Holy Scripture without filtering both through our own experience, nor should we.

When I read about the Israelites' wilderness journey, I think about our people. When you read the texts, do you not think about our ancestors' expressions upon hearing the text for themselves on Sunday evening as they worshipped in the slave quarters after having worked for the Master in the scathing sun or the frost-bite winters, getting by on little or nothing yet **somehow** holding on to the promises of God? Imagine, if you will, the look in their eyes as they allowed themselves to think about their bodies being freed just as God had freed their spirits.

The Word of God informs us, and our life experiences re-form the texts to make them relevant to our experience and relevant to our beliefs and our social location. In other words, the Word in its universal application can also speak specifically to a particular situation.

God sets in motion a liberating, supernatural faith that can overcome all things we live through. It jumps off the pages of Scripture for those who believe. In other words, when I begin to believe freedom is available to me because of God's mighty acts in the Bible, then liberation theology—the study of a God who seeks to deliver and set free from bondage—is a threat to those who have tried so long and so hard to keep me oppressed. Liberation theology, and Black liberation theology in particular, is an act of freedom. In that, freedom is the ability to explore all opportunities afforded by God. In the freedom of accepting God's invitation to know better, do better, and be better, we then resist one of life's greatest temptations: settling.

And you know when we are most tempted to settle, don't you?—when we are desperate!

This is where we find the Israelites in the seventeenth chapter of Exodus. The people are so desperate to quench their thirst with a bottle of Deer Park™ that they threaten Moses' life and wish themselves back in Egypt. What the people fail to realize is that the water they most desperately need is the living water of faith that only God provides. Despite Moses' warnings, the people seem oblivious to anything but the thirst in their throats.

Church, our time to be the Church is now despite the fact that we are living with desperate times lodged in our throats. We are thirsty, and we have every reason to be desperate and just settle. We have every reason to bicker and quarrel among each other like the Israelites. We could easily find ourselves in Rephidim, a place of no relief. No water. No hope. Settling in such a state of desperation, we would be oblivious to anything but the thirst in our throats.

Here's the good news! Today Moses shows us when we call on the name of the Lord under the pressures of desperate times, God brings relief. So Moses cried out to the Lord, "What shall I do with this people? They are almost ready to stone me!" Look at the instructions God gives in verse 5: "Go on ahead of my people," God says.

Church, to be an agent of change for justice in this community we must take the lead and make the decision to go it alone if necessary, not for selfish gain, but with the understanding that God has called us for such a time as this! Things are much better for most of us than they were for the Friendship 9. Shall we dare do less to make a difference than they did? You can answer that on your way home.

The second instruction God gives Moses is, "You are to take some of the elders with you." This is important to leaders in the Church and the community. When God calls you to serve, you are to be selective about who will join you in the mission. The elders of the Old Testament were seasoned, levelheaded, faithful, committed, and disciplined. All elders were older persons, but not all older persons were elders. So, when God calls you to a mission, be wise and discern who is to surround you. Ask yourself, "Do I know them to be people of integrity? Do I know them to operate under the authority of God?" Those answers can make the difference in the ministry succeeding or stalling or failing.

The next instruction God gives Moses is, "Take in your hand the staff with which you struck the Nile, and go." Here God directs Moses to use the tools God has given for the purpose and benefit of the entire community. You understand the staff itself has no power, but the staff in the hand of Moses—one who follows and obeys the word of the Lord—holds a divine, omnipotent presence.

As you will recall from Exodus 4, God calls Moses, and Moses already has the staff in his hand. God tells him to throw the staff on the ground, and when he does, the staff becomes a snake. God then tells Moses to pick up the snake by its tail, and when he does, the snake is transformed back into the staff. (*Are you with me?*) With this staff, Egyptian waters become blood. With this staff, streams of water birth a flood of frogs. With this staff, dust becomes lice. When stretched out toward heaven, this staff creates hail. When the staff is stretched out over the land, locusts spring up. All of this happens by the power of God.

God has the capacity to take what we already possess—our everyday tools of life—and use them to perform miracles right before our eyes for God's glory. God tools and re-tools God's people for the betterment of the Church, our community, and the world. Just as God calls Moses to lead God's people to the Promised Land, and to strike the rock in order to save the people from perishing, so God calls us to use our possessions— our time, our talents, our resources, our gifts, our faith and love of God and neighbor—to answer the cries of the needy, to bring political power to our people, to stand for justice, and to speak the truth in love!

God is calling us to pick up our staffs and strike the rock. Pick up your staff and strike the rock for justice. Pick up your staff, strike the rock, and "let justice roll down like a river, righteousness like a never-failing stream!" Pick up your staff and go to the rock—not the rock in Massah and Meribah. Go to *the* Rock, the stone the builders rejected, the Rock of Ages. Jesus is the rock! Only Jesus sets us free from our complacency, liberates us from the political scare tactics of our enemies, and empowers us to see a brand new day. Only Jesus can right the wrongs of this world through our hands and feet. So, go to *the* Rock!

We are a liberated people. We are a free people. We are an empowered people, not because of the work of the Friendship 9, Martin, Malcolm, Shirley, or President Obama. Not even because of Moses. We are a liberated people because we have been in contact with the Divine Liberator. We are a free people because of our covenant relationship with the Triune God, our Freedom Fighter. Because of Jesus, we are no longer enslaved to sin but we are saved, delivered, and set free. Because of Jesus, troubled waters are transformed into cleansing baptismal pools, and we experience God's justifying grace. Because of Jesus, the chains are broken because God is in the midst. Because of Jesus, generational curses cease to steal, kill, and destroy our community. At the name of Jesus, the anointing falls, reconciliation is a done deal, and we no longer have to be divided by powers and principalities of this world.

So today, when times are desperate for so many, I stopped by to remind you that now is not the time for us to give up on God. We've got to press on. You've got to make your way to the Rock with a staff in hand. We've got to take what we've got to get the justice we want! I dare you to strike the Rock, tap into the power source, and watch God turn some things upside down. Watch God turn your situation around. Watch God give you signs and perform wonders. Despite all of the bad news, there is still the power of the Good News. Despite the pain and the disappointment, I know deep in my soul that God is on our side. Despite how things look right now, I know that God is working it all out. Through many dangers, toils, and snares we have already come, and we've come too far to turn back now. I believe somebody's gonna' stand on the Rock of Ages. Will you hold on until it comes to pass? I heard somebody say, "Yeah!" Yeah! Yeah.

And it is so. In the name of the Father, the Son, and the Holy Spirit. Amen.

The Anatomy of a Dream

Eustacia Moffett Marshall

BIO. IN BRIEF

Reverend Eustacia Moffett Marshall serves as the Campus
Minister of the St. James Presbyterian Church in Greensboro,
North Carolina. She is a published writer. Rev. Moffett Marshall
received her Bachelor of Arts Degree from Stanford University
and a Master of Divinity Degree from Princeton Theological
Seminary, where she graduated with academic distinction,
receiving eight academic awards. Rev. Marshall is an acting
board of trustee member for the Presbyterian Foundation, an
advisory member of the African American Advisory Council of
the Presbyterian Church, and the most recent chair of the Bills
and Overtures Committee of the 220th General Assembly.

**Genesis 37:3-5, 19-20, 23-25; 39:1-4
(New Revised Standard Version)**

*Now Israel loved Joseph more than any other of his children, because
he was the son of his old age; and he had made him a long robe with
sleeves. But when his brothers saw that their father loved him more
than all his brothers, they hated him, and could not speak peaceably
to him. Once Joseph had a dream, and when he told it to his brothers,*

*they hated him even more. … They said to one another, "Here comes
this dreamer. Come now, let us kill him and throw him into one of the
pits; then we shall say that a wild animal has devoured him, and we
shall see what will become of his dreams." … So when Joseph came to
his brothers, they stripped him of his robe, the long robe with sleeves
that he wore; and they took him and threw him into a pit. The pit was
empty; there was no water in it. Then they sat down to eat; and looking
up they saw a caravan of Ishmaelites coming from Gilead, with their
camels carrying gum, balm, and resin, on their way to carry it down
to Egypt.*

---

*Now Joseph was taken down to Egypt, and Potiphar, an officer
of Pharaoh, the captain of the guard, an Egyptian, bought him from
the Ishmaelites who had brought him down there. The LORD was with
Joseph, and he became a successful man; he was in the house of his
Egyptian master. His master saw that the LORD was with him, and that
the LORD caused all that he did to prosper in his hands. So Joseph found
favor in his sight and attended him; he made him overseer of his house
and put him in charge of all that he had.*

It will be no surprise to you when I say that people do give
up on dreams. Circumstances can deflate our dreams the
way a pin deflates a balloon, and it is possible to become
cynical, skeptical, distrustful, and doubtful that our dreams
will come to pass. Given the stress and strains of our current
economic condition, the crisis of our educational system, the
cradle-to-prison pipeline funding private corporations, and
the disproportionate ways in which our country continues to
help the rich and hurt the poor, it takes an enormous amount
of work for us to keep a dream alive. Given our current reality,
we can be tempted to render our dreams dead.

Dr. Michelle Alexander, author of *The New Jim Crow: Mass
Incarceration in the Age of Colorblindness*, makes a compelling

observation that today there are more African Americans in prison or jail, on probation or parole than were enslaved in 1850, a decade before the Civil War began.[1] Today our community is in a state of emergency. And how important it is that the body of Christ is revived and energized to be a Church that gets up, gets out, and gets to work towards the vision of justice God has for the world. Today, more African American males are unable to vote (due to felony laws) than in 1870, the year the Fifteenth Amendment passed which prohibits laws denying the right to vote based on race.

While God is calling our nation to realize a dream of justice and equality, and while we celebrate the progress we have made, the truth is, for every two steps forward, it seems we have taken two steps back. It takes an enormous amount of work for us to keep a dream alive.

Dreams for a better world, dreams for a better nation, dreams for a better community, dreams for a better Church, dreams for ourselves, are often threatened and discouraged by the reality of where we are now. We thought we would be up, but we find ourselves down. We thought we would be advancing, but we find ourselves regressing. And the frustration of where we are, and the pain of not being where we know God would have us to be, can leave us feeling wiped out and worn out, let down, put down, and perhaps even beat down to the point where we might believe that our dreams have fallen apart, disappeared, gone up in flames! So today, I want to suggest to you that given our reality, we will think our dreams are falling apart, unless we understand the *anatomy of a dream*.

When we think of the word anatomy, we often think of the human body. Anatomy has to do with how something is shaped and formed for living. Just as you and I have an anatomy as humans, dreams have an anatomy too. Dreams are formed and shaped to come to life. And the Joseph story helps us understand how dreams come to life. **Dreams come to life in broken places.**

Joseph of our text was part of a broken family. The scripture says that Joseph's father, Israel, loves Joseph more than he loves any of his children. And because Joseph is his father's favorite, sibling rivalry kicks in to the point where Joseph's brothers hate him and cannot stand to talk to him. Because Joseph enjoys a special relationship with his father, he is the brunt of his brothers' jokes and the outcast of brotherly affection. He is talked about, left out, and put out. By favoring one child over another, Joseph's father has created a dysfunctional family. And if you read Genesis 37 carefully, you will see that Joseph, being the teacher's pet, his father's favorite, is a tattle-tell, braggadocios, perhaps even obnoxious at times brother. But no matter how flawed Joseph is, you can imagine that Joseph does not like being on the outs of his brothers' affection. It is in the midst of this broken family that God births a dream through Joseph.

In the dream, Joseph foresees his brothers bowing down to him. In other words, Joseph begins to imagine a reality very different from the one he is in. I just told you that dreams come to life in broken places. You see, we have dreams because we are imagining a reality different from the messed-up place we are in. The dream is evidence that we are reaching and striving for something different, something more, and something better.

And this is not just a lesson learned from Joseph; this is also the lesson learned from other dreamers in all times, spaces, and places. Dreamers like François-Dominique Toussaint Louverture, the leader of the Haitian revolution who declared he may have been born a slave, but he possessed the soul of a free man.[2] Although he lived in a broken nation, ruled by the colonial powers of the French and Spanish, he dreamed of a free nation, and he had the military genius and the political acumen to establish the independent black country of Haiti. Dreams come alive in broken places.

Ella Baker saw the brokenness of a democracy that did not allow the voices of all the people. She dreamed of a country that was participatory and included everybody. So she helped to found the Southern Christian Leadership Conference and the Student Non-Violent Coordinating Committee to fight racist policies and laws. Dreams come alive in broken places.

Tawakul Karman, a 32-year-old mother of three and chair of Women Journalists Without Chains in Yemen, sees the brokenness of government that allows 40% of the 23 million Yemen citizens to live on $2 a day or less, and she is leading a peaceful revolution to change her government. Dreams come to life in broken places!

And that is good news from the Lord because that tells us that our dysfunctional environments, our messed-up situations, our broken conditions are not a sign that the dream has been denied; it's actually confirmation that the dream is still alive. When we understand the anatomy of a dream (that is, that dreams take their shape and form in broken places), we will not be so quick to say that our dreams are falling apart. Though the dream is delayed, it need not be denied.

Next, Joseph's brothers try to kill his dream by throwing Joseph in a pit. But they cannot kill the dream. If they understood the anatomy of a dream, they would have known that pits do not destroy dreams. **In fact, the anatomy of a dream is such that dreams are strengthened in pits.**

Joseph's brothers say, "Come now, let us kill Joseph and throw him into one of the pits . . . and we shall see what will become of his dreams. "The Bible says, ". . . they took him and threw him into a pit. The pit was empty; there was no water in it." I don't have to tell you that being placed in a pit is difficult. But to add pain to injury, the scripture says there was no water in the pit. In the pit, it's just Joseph and the dream he carries. Joseph and his dream are not supposed to live because the text says there is no water in the pit. Without water, we can't live. But what we see is that Joseph and his dream do not die in the pit. They are kept alive. There is no water and he is in a pit. He is sent to the pit to die, but Joseph is kept alive. How does he stay alive?

He stays alive because somehow he learns to live without water. Somehow he learns to live through thirsty conditions. He can't reach water to satisfy and strengthen him, so he learns how to pull on an internal fountain of strength. And the Bible doesn't say what Joseph was doing down in the pit to tap into that internal fountain of strength, but I have a sneaky suspicion that Joseph was doing something to stay alive. What was he doing down in that pit? My preaching imagination was sparked when I read the word **pit**. The brothers threw him in a pit.

It is not a grave they threw him in; it's a pit. And there is a difference between a pit and a grave. A grave is a hole in the ground that is covered. A pit is a hole in the ground that has an opening. So when Joseph looked around in his pit, he was surrounded by darkness, but when he looked up, he could see some light. Even if his brothers threw Joseph in the pit at night, Joseph would still see the light of the moon and the stars. In the pit, he may not have water, but he has some light. In the pit, he can see light beyond his darkness. In that pit, it must have been that Joseph was looking up at whatever spec of light he could find, and his looking up kept him up. His looking up strengthened him.

Not too long ago, I learned how looking up can strengthen us. I had the privilege of being part of a leadership academy for pastors. During our inaugural retreat, my colleagues and I spent five days in the North Carolina Pisgah National Forest where we camped in the wilderness. It was a week filled with challenges because we were in the wild. There were no bathrooms. No beds. No kitchens. No cell phones. No computers. We couldn't even take deodorant with us. It was a week filled with challenges, and the week culminated with a high-ropes course forty feet above ground. Walking on any kind of tightrope suspended in mid-air is not my cup of tea. I worried about this challenge all week long. And to make matters worse, the day we were scheduled for the walk on the rope course is the day we woke up to gray skies and the pitter-patter of rain. So here I am, preparing to walk the slippery ropes. I'm in my red hat and my yellow rain coat. My stomach is turning. My heart is beating loud like a bass drum. My mind is moving quicker than the scrolling headlines on CNN. It's my turn to walk. I am scared because when I look below me all I can see is a 40-foot fall. When I look behind me, all I can see is fog. When I look in front of me, all I can see is an unsteady, shaky, slippery rope. I felt shut in, locked in, fenced in, hemmed in, blocked in, and closed in. I had reached my pit 40 feet in the air and truth is I almost let go until the Lord spoke to me. The Lord said, "If you are going to make it through this, you can't look down, you can't look behind, and you can't look in front of you, but you must look up." And when I looked up, I could see the harness above me. The harness above me was connected to the equipment I was wearing. And this harness apparatus was holding me up.

The rain was still falling, the ropes were still shaky, but the sight of the harness above me connected to the hook gave me the strength to make it through. No matter how difficult the challenge, looking up was enough to keep me standing. Looking up was enough to keep me walking. Looking up was enough to keep my spirit from despair because I knew that what was above me was protecting me! I knew that what was above me was holding on to me! Looking up kept me up!

Is there anybody here who can say I may feel locked in, fenced in, hemmed in, blocked in, and closed in a pit today, but I'm not buried. I may be in a pit, but I'm still alive. And as long as I look up, I can get to where I'm going. As long as I can look up, I can still see God moving. As long as I can look up, I can still see the protective mercies of the Master's hand. And that gives me strength. Looking up will keep you up!

Pits can cause you to lift your eyes up, to throw your hands up, and to call on the strength of the Lord. In fact, every now and then when I look over my life, I don't just thank God for mountain moments, I thank him for the pits, because in the pits I learned how to trust the Lord! In the pit, my faith grew stronger! In the pit, I grew a little wiser! In the pit, I learned humility! In the pit, I learned about a peace that the world can't give and the world can't take away! In the pit, I gained a greater resolve to serve the Lord. In the pit, I became more committed to work towards the dream! What didn't break me made me bolder. What didn't destroy me developed me. What didn't finish me fortified me. What didn't ruin me raised me. What didn't kill me made me stronger!

Joseph's brothers throw him in a pit, but if they understood the anatomy of a dream, they would have known that pits do not destroy dreams. The anatomy of a dream is such that dreams are strengthened in pits. **But not only are dreams strengthened in pits; the anatomy of a dream is such that they are sustained in pain.**

You can hurt a dreamer, but you can't kill a dream, not a God-given dream. The scripture lets us know that Joseph was taken from the pit and sold into the hands of Ishmaelites who were going down to Egypt. In Egypt, Joseph becomes human property in Potiphar's house. So Joseph goes from being stuck in a pit to being sold by his brothers into the Egyptian slave trade. The same brothers he saw in a dream bearing adoration for him are the ones who sell him into slavery. By all appearances, it looks as if Joseph's dream has certainly imploded.

Joseph is somebody else's property in Egypt. There, he finds himself in a painful situation where he has to wrestle with the contradiction of where he is and where God would have him to be. We as a people know about being sold by our brothers into slavery and we know what it's like to have to wrestle with the contradiction of where we are and where God would have us to be. We were created to be children of God, but we worked as people's property. We were good enough to fight in the Civil War, but we were still treated as second-class citizens during and after the war. In Reconstruction, we were promised 40 acres and a mule, but we only got ridicule and bad schools. We've had to live through some painful contradictions. But the good news is that dreams are sustained in pain. I know because the text says that in Egypt, the place where Joseph was considered the property of somebody else, in Egypt, the place where Joseph was never meant to survive, in Egypt, the text says, "the LORD was with Joseph and be became a successful man." That tells us that the evil plans of humans cannot destroy the plans of God because they cannot limit the power of God.

We may go through some pain, but the good news is that the dream is still preserved in the process. When Barack Obama took his oath on the steps of the White House the first time, I found myself reflecting on the fact that those same steps were built on the backs of African slaves. Our African ancestors were told that they were nothing and they would never amount to anything. But I have a sneaky suspicion that some mama working in the White House laundry, some daddy working on those White House steps, knew that with God all things are possible. I have a suspicion that some grandmamma, some granddaddy knew that the evil plans of humans couldn't destroy a dream birthed by God.

Folks may try to discourage a dream, folks may try to destroy a dream, folks will even inflict tortuous pain to stop a dream, but you can't kill a dream, not a God-given dream. Dreams are sustained in pain. And this is good news because there are a whole lot of reports on the pain that our world is enduring. CNN has its reports. MSNBC has their reports. FOX News has its reports. Wall Street has their reports, the creditors have their reports, your children have their reports, our spouses have their reports, but I'm here to let you know that there is another headline. Here's how it reads, "Now unto him who is able to keep you from falling…"[3] There is another headline! "If God is before you, who can be against you."[4] There is another headline! "The LORD is our refuge and strength, a very present help in times of trouble."[5] There is another headline! "They that wait on the LORD shall renew their strength, they shall mount on wings like eagles, they shall run and not grow weary; they shall walk and not grow faint."[6] There is another headline! "No weapon formed against you shall prosper."[7] There is another headline! "Many are the afflictions of the righteous but the LORD delivers them from them all!"[8] Dreams are sustained in pain.

Joseph's brothers throw him in a pit and sell him into slavery, trying to kill the dream and the dreamer. If they understood the anatomy of a dream, they would have known that pits do not destroy dreams, nor are dreams destroyed by pain. **The anatomy of a dream is such that dreams are strengthened in pits, dreams are sustained in pain, and finally dreams can sprout wherever we're planted.**

Though Joseph was living as somebody else's property in Egypt, our text says, "His master saw that the LORD was with him, and that the LORD caused all that he did to prosper in his hands. So Joseph found favor in his sight and attended him; he made him overseer of his house and put him in charge of all that he had."

Joseph experienced the pit and the pain of living as property in Potiphar's house. Later he will even go to prison before he sees the fulfillment of his dream. But on the way to his dream being fulfilled, one thing I love about Joseph is that he doesn't let his pit or his pain hinder his performance. In every place, whether he is in the pit or in Potiphar's house, Joseph still holds onto his dream. And Joseph uses the gifts God has given him to sprout, to grow where he is planted. This is the testimony of our foreparents in faith.

Martin Luther King Jr. was the pastor of a small congregation in a Jim Crow Alabama with a tiny office in the shadows of downtown Montgomery, but he led a bus boycott that spiraled into a worldwide movement. Dreams sprout where planted.

Mary McCloud Bethune only had one dollar and fifty cents starting out, but with it, during some of the roughest racist and sexist moments in America, she started Bethune Cookman College. Dreams sprout where planted. Fannie Lou Hamer was a sharecropper in Ku-Klux-Klan-riddled Mississippi; she only had a sixth-grade education, but she fought so courageously for black folk to vote that today we're still quoting Fannie Lou, not the Klan. Dreams sprout where planted. Shirley Chisholm was a black woman without the political capital of her counterparts, but in 1972 she became the first African American (male or female) from a major political party to run for President. Dreams sprout where planted.

I learned this lesson well while pregnant with my first child. One of the joys I experienced while being pregnant was receiving weekly e-mail updates on how the baby's anatomy was developing in preparation for birth. Each week I received a message about how the baby was being formed—from his brain, his heart, his eyes, his sense of smell, his hearing, to the growth of his little fingernails. All of these things are part of a baby's anatomy.

One week, as I was getting my weekly e-mail update, my son began to speak to me from the womb. I heard him saying, "Mommy, you are always getting excited about my growing anatomy." I said, "Yes, I sure am!" The baby said, "Well, I also want you to get excited about the womb. All of my development takes place in the womb. And even though the womb is a dark place and the temperature is very high in here, these are exactly the conditions God is using to develop me for birth. So as long as I'm up in here, I might as well sprout where I have been planted!"

I don't think my son is the only one who knows what a womb feels like. Somebody can look back over your life (you may not have to look too far) and see when you are were in a dark place where the heat was on. But thanks be to God, your conditions did not destroy you or your dreams! Someone may be in the fire right now, but you can look up from that pit, you can be sustained in that pain. God will use your circumstances to birth something in you, so you might as well sprout where you have been planted!

Well, my baby didn't stop speaking. He said, "Mommy, another reason why I'm cool with the womb is because I recognize that though it may seem like I'm up in here by myself, I've discovered that you are carrying me wherever you go." I said, "Boy, you just gave me the close for my sermon." The Bible says, "*The Lord was with Joseph,*" and is there anybody here who can testify that you have been in some dark places? You've been in some heat. You've had your share of pits and you have gone through some show-nuff pain. But on your journey, *the Lord has been with you.* The Lord has never failed you. The Lord has never left you. The Lord made a way. You can say, "I was in the pit and in some pain, but I'm standing on my feet today as a testimony that I survived because the Lord was with me. This is our testimony. I should have given up in the Middle Passage, but the Lord was with me. I should have given up through 244 years of slavery, but the Lord was with me. I should have let go through Jim and Jane crow, but the Lord was with me. And because the Lord is with me, the dream is still alive. It lives in the eyes of our seniors. It lives in the hopes of our youth. It lives in me! It lives in you! The dream is still alive because Jesus is still alive!"

And we know what happened to Jesus. They nailed him to a cross, trying to kill a dream. They put Jesus in a tomb, trying to kill a dream. But on the third day, Jesus sprouted where he was planted! Jesus rose from the dead as evidence that you can't kill a dream! And I'm so glad he lives. Because Jesus lives, I've got hope for tomorrow. Because he lives, I still have joy in my sorrow. Because he lives, the dream lives. Pits can't destroy it. Pain can't terminate it.

Thank God for the anatomy of a dream!

NOTES

1. Michelle Alexander, *The New Jim Crow: Mass Incarceration in the Age of Colorblindness* (New York, NY: The New Press, 2010), 176.

2. See http://toussaintlouverturehs.org for complete information on the life and achievements of Toussaint Louverture.

3. Jude 1:24, RSV.

4. Romans 8:31, RSV.

5. Psalm 46:1, RSV.

6. Isaiah 40:31, RSV.

7. Isaiah 54:17, RSV.

8. Psalm 34:19, RSV.

Criminal Minds

Gloria E. Miller

BIO. IN BRIEF

Reverend Dr. Gloria E. Miller is a graduate of Trinity College
in Washington, D.C., where she served as the first Protestant
Chaplain for the College. She holds a Master of Divinity Degree
from Howard University School of Divinity. In 2013, she earned
the Doctorate of Ministry degree from Regent University in
Virginia Beach, Virginia, graduating summa cum laude. Her
concentration was Christian Leadership and Renewal. From
1999 to 2002, she served as Chief of Staff/Senior Assistant at
Metropolitan Baptist Church, in Washington, D.C.
Since 2002, she has served as Associate Pastor at the
First Baptist Church of Glenarden in Landover, Maryland.

Luke 23:39-43 (New King James Version)
*Then one of the criminals who were hanged blasphemed Him, saying,
"If You are the Christ, save Yourself and us."*

*But the other, answering, rebuked him, saying, "Do you not even
fear God, seeing you are under the same condemnation? And we indeed
justly, for we receive the due reward of our deeds; but this Man has
done nothing wrong." Then he said to Jesus, "Lord, remember me when
You come into Your kingdom."*

And Jesus said to him, "Assuredly, I say to you, today you will be with Me in Paradise."

Many of you may be familiar with the series "Criminal Minds," where a team of profilers from the FBI's Behavioral Analysis Unit seek to profile and find criminals who have committed horrific crimes. "Criminal Minds" differs from many procedural dramas by focusing on the criminal rather than the crime.

I thought about this show in connection with my text, where two criminals are being crucified with Jesus. The scene is set. Just before the noon hour, Jesus is hanging on the cross, with one criminal on His right and one criminal on His left. The crowd, looking on, the rulers and the soldiers, all began to mock Jesus. Their scorn, today, would be equal to cussing someone out.

They tried to depict Jesus as someone He was not; they tried to make Him a criminal. They tried to make this innocent man guilty by falsely accusing Him of a crime He did not commit. We see this played out every day, trying to make the innocent guilty and the guilty innocent. Nothing has changed in over 2,000 years. The more things change, the more they stay the same.

All four of the Gospels note the fact that there were two criminals with Christ, but only Luke's Gospel zeroes in to give an account of what was happening among the three. I started to think about what may have been going on in the minds of these two criminals as they hung on their crosses with Jesus in the middle. Now, I don't claim to be a criminal profiler. I have never engaged in the study of criminal minds, but I believe with a little investigation we can learn what was on their minds. The more I thought about this as I used my spiritual imagination, I concluded that the way to know what was on the minds of the two criminals was to listen closely to what they were saying as they hung on their crosses. It has been said that you can learn a great deal about a person by the words that come out of his or her mouth. In fact, the writer Mark Twain said, "Better to remain silent and be thought a fool than to speak out and remove all doubts." Your words can reveal a great deal about you.

Now in order to frame my discussion of these criminal minds, we start with the premise that thoughts are produced by the brain. The Hebrew writers understood the mind (the brain) as the inner being of a person—much like the heart. In the New Testament when the writers spoke of a person's mind, it was mostly in connection with a person's heart. The mind and heart are often spoken of synonymously in the Scriptures. Jesus connected the heart and mind too: "You shall love the Lord your God with all your heart, with all your soul, and with all your mind."[1]

A person's actions flow from the inclinations of his or her mind. Whether a person does good or evil depends on the state of that person's mind/heart. Solomon, a man of great wisdom, said in Proverbs 4:23: "Keep your heart with all diligence, for out of it springs the issues of life." Paul's writings make it clear that the condition of the mind will determine whether a person is controlled by the flesh or by the Spirit (see Romans 8:6-7). A person's mind that is dominated by the gods of this world will have their minds darkened or covered as if a veil has been placed over them. That's what Paul says. For instance, when we see people killing other people as if they were playing a video game and seemingly having no remorse, we know that their minds have been darkened; they're veiled. But, when our minds are transformed and renewed by the power of God and His word, there is a change in our behavior. We move from the darkness into the marvelous light.

Now, let's look as these two criminals and eavesdrop on their conversation to find out what was on their minds. **First, I want to suggest that one criminal had contempt on his mind.** Listen to him. The text says he "blasphemed Jesus." He spoke words of disdain, disregard, and dislike against Jesus. He spoke words of contempt. Next, notice if you will, this criminal made a demand on Jesus: "If you are the Christ, save yourself and save us." In the ancient text, it reads, "Art thou the Christ?" In other words, he was saying to Jesus, "Aren't you the Man? Do your thing." If you are who you claim to be, get us out of this mess. He did not show regard for Jesus' suffering and agony, just blatant contempt.

It's like people who see you at your weakest moment in your walk with God and say, "You're supposed to be Christian…" They look down on you with contempt. And their contempt usually comes into play because they don't want to take responsibility for their behavior, so they try to turn the spotlight on you. In Psychology 101, this is called transference. You transfer your behavior to me. You try to make yourself look good by making me look bad. An Amen goes right there.

This first criminal did not want to pay his debt for his deeds. He did not want to be accountable for his actions or take responsibility for his behavior. Don't you know people like that? People want to get out of their mess, by any means necessary. You know persons like that, don't you. They may be sitting in your seat. It does not matter who they hurt in the process. They just want out of their mess.

This first criminal spoke words of contempt because he was self-centered and concerned about his welfare. This criminal was not concerned about Jesus being saved from His suffering. It was all about this criminal trying to save his life. He was self-focused, self-centered. How do you know if you are self-focused or self-centered? When **you** are always on **your** mind. This man had broken the law of the land, yet he did not want to be punished for his crime. In his heart there was no remorse, there were no words of repentance, just contempt for Jesus not doing for him what he wanted done. It was all about him.

This man was busy talking down to Jesus instead of standing up and taking responsibility for his actions. Many criminals don't want to be held accountable for their crimes. Most criminals plead not guilty in a court of law. They are looking for a way out. One of my favorite lines from the movie *Shawshank Redemption* was when Andy asks Red, who was played by Morgan Freeman, what he was in for. Red replied, "Don't you know we are all innocent in here?"

We all have to own our stuff. The enemy works hard on our minds to prevent us from facing and taking responsibility for our truth because he knows the truth will set us free. He works overtime trying to keep us from facing our realities. He fills our minds with all kinds of garbage and false information to the point that many of us can hardly tell right from wrong. We are too busy trying to live in the grey areas of life.

At some point, we have to face the truth of our situations and turn our focus on Jesus. This first criminal could not see Jesus in his midst because he was too busy focusing on himself. Sometimes we can be in the presence of Jesus and not recognize Him, because our focus is on ourselves. Only when we take the focus off of ourselves can we see Jesus.

Now, before we become too judgmental of this first criminal, let's look in the mirror. Let me ask you, what laws have you broken? Who have you robbed? Who have you cheated? From whom have you stolen? Whom have you told a lie on? What crimes have you committed? How many red lights did you run this week? How much have you stolen from your job? (Yeah, those note pads and paper clips count too.) How many times have you been given too much change from the clerk, and did not give it back? What tricks did you play on your income taxes this year? How much of a criminal are you? I think I'm in the house!

Mama's theology said, "Sin is sin no matter who it's in." We are quick to categorize and minimize our sins by looking at other people. Too many of us justify our behavior by saying I am not as bad as certain people are. Our remorse for our behavior, if any, is not that we have done wrong, but that we were caught. We are all guilty at some point.

Your mug shot may not be on the post office wall. But you know and God knows where you have fallen short. Not every crime is solved. Not every criminal is brought up on charges. Not every guilty person goes to jail. There are many cold cases that have not been cracked. Not every murderer is on death row. In fact, there may be one on your row. How often have we missed the mark? We need to take our eyes off others and look in the mirror.

You know what this is like? It's like when you go to the gas station to buy some gas. You swipe your card, push the debt or credit button, push all the other buttons, put in your zip code, press the button for the type of gas you want, do you want a receipt. You know the drill. You open the gas tank, put in the hose, and click the handle and nothing comes out.

You keep trying without any success. So you have to go into the store (I hate that part) and tell the clerk your pump is not working. The clerk comes out with you, only to find that there is nothing wrong with the pump—the hose is twisted. The gas can't flow through the line because the hose is twisted. Come on somebody.

That's what happens to us when our thinking is out of line with the Word of God. Our minds are twisted. Some of us have been blocking the flow of God into our lives and now our minds are twisted. We let our minds think as the world thinks, rather than how God thinks. We start to tilt the scale and it does not matter who gets thrown under the bus when our minds are twisted. The first criminal spoke words of contempt for Jesus because his mind was twisted. Our actions are a direct result of our thoughts. When you have a negative mind, you will have a negative life. The battle is in the mind. The first criminal spoke a word of contempt because he was self-centered, he refused to take responsibility for his actions, and his mind was twisted. I'm talking about criminal minds.

The second criminal spoke a word of confession. Now, I want to note that the scripture says in Matthew's Gospel that in the beginning, "even the two criminals crucified next to Jesus joined in the mockery."[2] Both criminals were shouting at Jesus in the beginning. They both wanted to be delivered from the excruciating pain and impending death. But somewhere in the middle of this discourse on the cross, seeing the shed blood of Jesus, and His broken body, there was a shift, a modification in the mind of the second criminal. He had a change of mind. He put the first criminal on blast, made him shut up, and said, "How dare you? We indeed have done wrong, and we deserve what we are getting. But, this man has done nothing wrong."

Here is an admission of guilt, a confession. This second criminal came to his senses. When he recognized who Jesus was, his thought process changed. He took the focus off of himself and made his confession. And the truth of the matter is that the only way we are invited to be in right relationship with Jesus Christ is that we confess when we are wrong.

Confession precedes forgiveness! 1 John 1:9 says, "If we confess our sins, He is faithful and just to forgive us our sins and cleanse us from all unrighteousness." This second criminal took ownership of his wrongdoing. Upon his confession, a transformation took place. He no longer had the mind of a criminal upon his confession. Salvation comes with confession. From that confession, he was in a place where his mind would be renewed, redeemed, and redirected by the saving grace of Jesus Christ. The second criminal changed his mind and in so doing, he changed his direction and he changed his destiny. He now has an all-access pass to heaven. He now has an express ticket. He was put on a non-stop flight to heaven to be with Jesus forever. His eternal future was changed because his mind was changed. The reality is that our minds determine our thoughts, and our thoughts determine our choices. And our choices will direct our actions. How we live out our lives is determined by the choices we make. Everything changed for the second criminal because he had a change of mind and confessed his sin.

Confession is good for the soul. Confession makes mercy possible. I don't know about you, but I need mercy. I need mercy so I don't get what I deserve. I believe an Amen goes there. When we confess our sins.... Ya'll don't hear me. When we admit that we have done wrong, Jesus saves us. Now, some of you ain't done nothin' wrong. You've been saved all of your life. But I was a sinner. Is there anyone in the house who was a sinner? Lying, stealing, and defaming the name of God. But one day, one day, one day, you had a little talk with Jesus. And He made it all right. He healed you, cleansed you, and made you whole. He changed your mind. He helped you to think right, so you could walk right, and then you could talk right, all because you made a confession of your sins.

But let me be true to the text. This second criminal did not make just one confession; he made two confessions. He confessed he was a sinner, and he confessed Jesus was Lord! The title Lord is significant here for a couple of reasons. First, he ascribes to Jesus a designation that was also being given to Caesar. Second, to call Jesus Lord was to call Him "God." When Thomas encountered Jesus the risen Christ, he stated publicly, "My Lord and my God."[3] Paul declared, "There is only one true God and one true Lord, Jesus Christ."[4] As transformation takes place in our minds and hearts, we elevate Jesus not only to the status of being our Savior but also our Lord.

This second criminal seized the moment. In the twinkling of an eye, there was a flash of recognition, a swift realization that brought about a resolution that moved the second criminal from the darkness of death to the radiant sunshine of hope and life. He had a change of mind. He changed his thoughts; and when his thoughts changed, his choices changed. He chose to see Jesus not as a criminal but as the Christ, as his Savior and Lord. His picture was taken off the post office wall and put into the hall of faith. Because he put his faith in the Righteous Judge, he was able to walk out of the courtroom free with a judgment of not guilty. His thinking changed, and because of that, he could rise to the level of his thoughts. The Bible says, "As a man thinketh in his heart, so is he."[5] When we confess our sins before Jesus the Christ and surrender our minds to Him, our thinking changes. This man's thinking changed. He no longer has a criminal mind. We are the product of our thinking. Your life will never change until your thinking changes. It all boils down to our thinking and to what we allow to rest in our minds.

Now I hear some of you saying, I know some people whose minds are jacked up; they have sinking thinking. And they have confessed Christ, they go to church every Sunday, pay their tithes, sing in the choir, usher on the usher board, lead a ministry and more for the Church. Well, I'm glad you raised this issue. Let me see if I can bring some clarity to this point. Right thinking is not the main determiner of one's salvation. Salvation is based solely on the blood of Jesus, His death on the cross, and His resurrection. Many people will be in heaven because they accepted Jesus as their Savior. But many of these same people will never walk in thorough victory or enjoy the totality of the good plan God has for their lives because they did not fully use the Word of God and the example of Christ in their lives.

Let me break it down this way. The truth is that before we met Jesus we were hopeless and miserable. Once we know him, if we refuse to surrender our minds to him, we are just miserable. And because we are miserable, we make wrong choices, and because we make wrong choices, we usually end up making other folks miserable. Victorious living in Christ starts with confession and a new mind-set. When we confess, we take on the mind of Christ. The Bible says, "Let this mind be in you which was also in Christ Jesus."[6] But to take on the mind of Christ, we need to know the Word which teaches us who Christ is and how to follow the example of Christ.

In God's order of things, right thinking comes first, and right actions follow. When we are thinking right, we are living our lives according to the ways of God and not the world. It does not take a lot of effort to let your mind drift from the ways of God. That is why we have to practice daily thinking like God and not the world. We need a clear vision so that we will know where to stand and what to stand for. The question we all need to answer is, "Am I single-minded or am I double-minded?" The second man did not waiver once he acknowledged Jesus as his LORD.

At the cross, there were words of contempt and words of confession. But, there was one more word spoken during this dialogue from the cross, which was **a word of certainty from One who knew no sin**. I can shout Hallelujah there! Jesus always has the final say! While in the depth of His own agony, Jesus assured the second criminal on the cross, "Today you will be with me in Paradise!" The Greek word Paradise *(paradeisos)* means garden or park. Revelation 22 describes it as a place with "a life-giving tree and living river." The old preacher said it was a place where we will study war no more, a place where the lion and the lamb will lay down together, a place where every day is Sunday and the Sabbath has no end, a place of honor, a place where we will experience eternal joy in the presence of our Savior and our Lord!

Jesus removed all doubt from the second criminal's mind by saying, "Today, Today, Tell your neighbor, Today." That word **today** is translated *NOW*! At this moment, it will happen. Not next month, not next week, not tomorrow, but TODAY! Jesus was saying surely it will happen. "Don't worry, be happy! Don't sweat it; it is going to happen. Chill Out! I am going to do it." Jesus was saying to this second criminal, "I got you covered. I got your back. I won't forget you. I won't leave you behind." This penitent criminal was to be with his dying and soon-to-be-resurrected Lord in paradise.

In the living of our lives, many people have made promises to us. Even in our churches, we may count a great number of people, but most often, there are only a few we can count on. In our relationships we have been abandoned, abused, and attacked by persons who we thought had our best interest at heart. We put our confidence in them, we felt certain they would do what they said they were going to do. We believed in their commitment to us, only to find out that when the rubber met the road they were as counterfeit as a three-dollar bill.

But when it is all said and done, no matter what we have been through in this life, we can always count on Jesus. If He said it, He will do it! Just as He assured the second criminal, He assures us that no matter what you been through if you put your trust in Him, He will not fail you!

Let me get out of here when I tell you this. The first criminal made a demand on Jesus, the second criminal made a request. The first criminal wanted to come down and the second criminal wanted to go up. The first criminal was looking for a temporary fix but the second criminal was looking for an eternal solution. These criminals provide several lessons for you and me. But the main lesson that we need to take home is that the day we acknowledge Jesus as our Savior, and repent of our sins, we have allowed Him to change our minds. Change our thinking! Change our talking! Change our walking! When we do this, we have the assurance that we will meet Jesus in Paradise. This is a word of promise. It is a promise you can take from earth to eternity because Jesus is the ultimate promise keeper.

One day, we will meet Him in paradise. It does not matter what life looks like now—Jesus always has the last word. He changes minds, even criminal minds! Anybody been changed? Was it an old-school change that you talk about the way Tramaine Hawkins sang about it: "A change, a change has come over me. He changed my life; a wonderful a wonderful change, has come over meeeeeeee." Or was it a new-school change that you talk about the way William McDowell sings about it: "I've been changed, healed, freed, delivered; I found joy, grace, and favor, and I've been changed. Today is the day, I've been changed."

Give God some praise if you have been changed! If you have made a confession, if you claim Jesus as Lord, if you know for certain you are on your way to Paradise, give God some praise! Thank you, Lord, for the change, the awe-inspiring change, the awesome change, the amazing change!

NOTES

1. Matthew 22:37, NKJV.
2. Matthew 27:44, NKJV.
3. John 20:28, NKJV.
4. 1 Corinthians 8:5-6, NKJV.
5. Proverbs 23:7, NKJV.
6. Philippians 2:5, NKJV.

Faith Walkers: Walk, Work, Witness, and Build for the Kingdom of God

Leslie Watson Malachi

BIO. IN BRIEF

Reverend Leslie Watson Malachi is the Director of African American Religious Affairs for People for the American Way. She is the former National Policy Director for the Balm In Gilead and the Director of the Multicultural Programs Department of the Religious Coalition for Reproductive Choice, where she co-authored two faith-based sexuality education dialogue models, "Keeping It Real!" for teens and "Breaking the Silence" for adults. She has provided training in grassroots organizing, strategic planning, and civic engagement. She is the Director of Advocacy for the Progressive National Baptist Convention, Inc. and serves as a member of the ministerial staff of the historic Pilgrim Baptist Church in northeast D.C.

Acts 11:1-14 (New King James Version)

Now the apostles and brethren who were in Judea heard that the Gentiles had also received the word of God. And when Peter came up to Jerusalem, those of the circumcision contended with him, saying, "You went in to uncircumcised men and ate with them!"

But Peter explained it to them in order from the beginning, saying: "I was in the city of Joppa praying; and in a trance I saw a vision, an object descending like a great sheet, let down from heaven by four corners; and it came to me. When I observed it intently and considered, I saw four-footed animals of the earth, wild beasts, creeping things, and birds of the air. And I heard a voice saying to me, 'Rise, Peter; kill and eat.' But I said, 'Not so, Lord! For nothing common or unclean has at any time entered my mouth.' But the voice answered me again from heaven, 'What God has cleansed you must not call common.' Now this was done three times, and all were drawn up again into heaven. At that very moment, three men stood before the house where I was, having been sent to me from Caesarea. Then the Spirit told me to go with them, doubting nothing. Moreover these six brethren accompanied me, and we entered the man's house. And he told us how he had seen an angel standing in his house, who said to him, 'Send men to Joppa, and call for Simon whose surname is Peter, who will tell you words by which you and all your household will be saved.'"

Acts 11:15-18 (The Message)

"So I started in, talking. Before I'd spoken half a dozen sentences, the Holy Spirit fell on them just as he did on us the first time. I remembered Jesus' words: 'John baptized with water; you will be baptized with the Holy Spirit.' So I ask you: If God gave the same exact gift to them as to us when we believed in the Master Jesus Christ, how could I object to God?"

Hearing it all laid out like that, they quieted down. And then, as it sank in, they started praising God. "It's really happened! God has broken through to the other nations, opened them up to Life!"

A llow me to share with you a few thoughts on the Lord's continued revelation as it relates to His plan for us. Specifically I'd like to talk about His process, His provisions, His purpose, and His peace. My subject is Faith Walkers: Walk, Work, Witness, and Build for the Kingdom of God.

An old dollar bill and an even older twenty-dollar bill arrived at a Federal Reserve Bank to be retired. "I've had a pretty good life," the $20 bill said. "I've been to Vegas, the finest restaurants in New York, and even on a Caribbean cruise." "You did have an exciting life," the dollar said. "Where have you been?" the $20 bill asked the dollar. "Oh, I've been to the Methodist church, the Baptist church, spent time with the Lutherans…" "Wait," the $20 bill interrupted. "What's a church?" Indeed, what is a church?

The book of Acts, attributed to Luke, a gentile Christian, informs us of the life, challenges, and work of the early Church. Throughout its chapters we see how the Holy Spirit was instrumental in providing guidance and wisdom. The journey, the faith walk of those men and women, the process of "go ye" into various locations (without an automobile, an airplane, train, or bus), but only with determination and faith, is beyond admirable.

The text in Acts 11, which began in chapter 10, chronicles a journey, a process for the Apostle Peter. In chapter 10, we know that he and a man named Cornelius, a prominent figure and a gentile, had visions where the Lord essentially facilitated a strategic, divine introduction for the two to come together. You do know our God is strategic, don't you?

I found it interesting that Cornelius had little conversation with Peter and immediately moved to obedience. Peter, on the other hand, one writer says, has a dialogue assuming he knows more about what is profane and unclean than the Lord. Nevertheless, the two men meet and the presence of the Lord is apparent. Peter shares the good news with the gentiles, and the Holy Spirit "fell upon all who heard the Word" in what some call the historical "Gentile Pentecost."

I'm talking about God's **process**. The word process refers to something proceeding, something going on that is marked by gradual change. The word is a verb. The process of life means seeing the approaching storm, being in the storm, coming out of the storm, taking a breath and looking up to see another approaching storm.

Let me make this plain. The **process** involves the internal storm of realizing the complexity of being made in the image of God, receiving the guidance of the Holy Spirit so you can speak in a way that welcomes and affirms, to then hear shock, disappointment, discouragement, go back to your Gethsemane garden and wrestle with your "cup" while strengthening the Hope that is in you, for all those who will respond to "whosoever will." The process involves trusting the process, this walk of faith, so that you are light in the darkness (in a storm if you will) that includes prejudice, stigma, and people in bondage.

Again, a **process** signifies something proceeding, some ongoing that is marked by gradual change. God's plan was and is a process. Black folk know about being in a process. Some of our history bears repeating:

- Our American process started in the Middle Passage (the years of enslavement);
- Then there was the Emancipation Proclamation and the 13th, 14th, and 15th Amendments to the U.S. Constitution;

- There was Reconstruction, The Abolitionist Movement, The Harlem Renaissance, The Talented Tenth, and The Back to Africa Movement;
- The process in the '50s was worked in the Supreme Court decision argued by future Supreme Court Justice Thurgood Marshall in Brown vs. Topeka Board of Education;
- The process during the '60s included the assassination of Dr. Martin Luther King Jr., Malcolm X, John and Robert Kennedy, the riots of 1964, the passage of the 1964 and 1965 Civil Rights Act, the War on Poverty, and the Vietnam War;
- In the '70s Colored, Negro, Afro-American, Black, African American people tried to work the process of Affirmative action, set-asides, and lived through supply side economics (Reaganomics);
- The '80s saw an emergence of new church burnings in the south, mass incarceration of Black men, HIV/AIDS, crack cocaine and maximum minimum prison sentences, the Black middle class (Cosby families), and the birth of the still-misunderstood Hip-Hop nation;
- The process of the '90s brought the Republican Revolution, the Contract "On" America, welfare became Temporary Assistance for Needy Families (TANF), a new law about discrimination in the workplace (the Texaco Case) occurred, there was hair on a coke can, the assassination of Tupac Shakur and Clarence "Biggie" Smalls, and Father Mandela was released after 27 years in prison; and
- The process of the new millennium was ushered in with the election of a president who was born to a Caucasian woman and an African Man—the first African American president of the United States.

My people, today, I can say to you, walk with the "Way Maker"! Engage in His **process**, take the journey, endure the storms, and trust that the rainbows will show up.

Next, in speaking of Peter's vision in Acts 11, one writer says the vision was repeated "because of the importance of the issue of prejudice and that God needed to free Peter from his racial bigotry." By sharing his vision with the church in Jerusalem, they too had to face the limitations they placed on God. There is an intense debate taking place. This was not a casual conversation—although I would submit nothing was casual during these times when it came to understanding the risen Christ. But can you see Peter standing before "the criticism of the circumcised believers"? Ever been in that position? Not with "circumcised believers" but with those who say no to your yes? And what about those undecided and lukewarm ones, with whom I just have a problem in general?

Isaiah 42:6 says, "I, the Lord, have called you to demonstrate my righteousness. I will take you by the hand and guard you and I will give you to my people, Israel, as a symbol of my covenant with them. And you will be a light to guide the nations." You have ordered steps, Peter! God had already provided what Peter would need for this assignment—His hand, His protection, and the symbol of His promise. Not only does God invite us to walk through a process, God makes **provisions** for us because God knows who will fight us.

I see God's **provisions** in what Dr. Martin Luther King Jr. would say was "the winds of change" that began to blow in the 1960s. Affirming Baptist Churches, I see the provisions He has made for you, for us, in the actions of those with courage who were disrespected, who went beyond hurt, pain, and rejection and worked with what they had for their walk. What were some of the provisions?

- Civil disobedience and community organizing from the '60s provided a strategy;
- The 1963 March on Washington work led by Bayard Rustin provided a paradigm;
- The first public protest by gays and lesbians at the White House in 1965 (Dr. Frank Kameny leading) showed there was conviction;
- Loving vs. Virginia in 1967 showed there was commitment;
- Stonewall Inn, Greenwich Village, New York in 1969 (the start of the US Gay Movement) provided organization;
- An enemy (the Religious Right, Christian Coalition formed in the '70s) provided commonality;
- The late Harvey Milk's election to the San Francisco Board of Supervisors in 1977 showed everyone had worth;
- The 1993 "Don't Ask, Don't Tell" Law showed who the targets were;
- The 1996 Defense of Marriage Act (DOMA), signed into law, gave us a cause;
- In 2007, New Hampshire, Oregon, and Washington legalized civil unions or domestic partnerships gave hope;
- In 2009, Proposition 8 (defining marriage between a man and a woman) caused us to rally;
- In 2009, the Matthew Shepard and James Byrd, Jr. Hate Crimes Prevention Act was fruit of our labor;
- In 2012, the EEOC ruling on job discrimination gave us energy;
- And the 2013 Supreme Court ruling on DOMA gave so many who had waited so long victory!

We know God has a process, one that is strategic, and so are His **provisions**. Many LGBTQ persons have accepted Jesus Christ as their Lord and Savior. God knew the day would come where ministry would change to consciously and consistently preach and teach without hurt or harm to anyone.

Peter might not have understood "why him," but the Lord provided clear directions for walking by faith and trusting in Him. Trust that just as He has provided, He will provide again, my friends. How do I know this? Because He has plans for us to prosper and to give us a future," says the Lord in Jeremiah 29:11. And He blesses us to be a blessing to others. I know it because you, the Association of Welcoming and Affirming Baptists, are here today celebrating, praising, and affirming that shows that "greater is He who is in you than he who is in the world."[1]

I challenge you to tell somebody when you leave here tonight, I trust and believe He has already provided for us, for this work, for this ministry to keep on empowering others, to keep on until injustice, intolerance, stigma, prejudice, homophobia, and stereotypes are no longer main concerns. I believe you can say as I do—I might have to wait, just a little while longer, but I am a witness to His **"on time, just what I need" provisions** for this walk, this journey!

Now, our passage moves us to the **purpose** of God. Acts 11:12-14 says, *"Just then three men who had been sent from Caesarea arrived at the house where we were staying. The Holy Spirit told me to go with them and not to worry that they were Gentiles. These six brothers here accompanied me, and we soon entered the home of the man who had sent for us. He told us how an angel had appeared to him in his home and had told him, 'Send messengers to Joppa, and*

*summon a man named Simon Peter. He will tell you how you and
everyone in your household can be saved!'"*

We are to walk through His process. We are to work with
His provisions. Then, we must **witness about His purpose**.
Walk, work, and witness for building up the Kingdom of God.
Hmmm. There is a song of old, not too old, that says, "When I
look back over my life…" I wonder if Peter may have felt like
Dr. King who said something like, "One day we will look back
on these times and see God working through history for the
salvation of men." These are listening, teaching, trusting times
of fellowship, devotion, and prayer. We are becoming stronger
witnesses with stronger testimonies. Bishop Joel Jacobs wrote,
"A testimony increases your vocabulary." I take that to mean
going from I, my, and me to we, our, and us.

Are you a witness to what God can do? Are you taking the
limits off God to go and tell everyone how they can be saved?
You can be a national witness. That's why:

- At least 14 states now have same sex marriage (5 by courts,
  6 by state legislatures, and 3 by popular vote);
- Trayvon Martin's legacy will not just be about what he
  wore or held that fateful night, but about Stand Your
  Ground laws moving from competing priorities to a
  significant priority;
- Voter Suppression equals needing proof of citizenship
  from everyone, but to paraphrase Genesis 50:20, "what
  man meant for harm, God means for good"; and
- Our voice can facilitate Supreme Court decisions that are
  for all the people, not a small group of people.

*"He will tell you how you and everyone in your household
can be saved!"* Did God say just the immediate family? Those
who had Roman citizenship? To some and not all? No! God

said witness to *everyone*—no one is to be lost and left behind. All who believe in their heart that Jesus Christ is Lord can be saved!

Faith walkers, I say to you in this time of jubilee, of celebration, continue to share and encourage, be encouraged so that when you approach a lost sheep, you can tell them about the Savior. Tell somebody that you are a **witness** to those who have been troubled on every side, but won't be crushed. A **witness** to somebody who has been perplexed, but not in despair; persecuted, but not abandoned by God; struck down, but not destroyed. Tell them that same person went through God's process, counted on His seen and unseen provisions, and became a **witness**, a voice for the voiceless, the battered, bruised, and the walking wounded.

His purpose is manifested through our individual and collective lives making you and me **witnesses**. So, tell your stories. Tell how you've seen people make it, how God has helped people make it, and most importantly, how God saved you because He has a **purpose** for your life.

Finally, verses 15-18 in chapter 11 in The Message translation reads, *"So I started in, talking. Before I'd spoken half a dozen sentences, the Holy Spirit fell on them just as he did on us the first time. I remembered Jesus' words: 'John baptized with water; you will be baptized with the Holy Spirit.' So I ask you: If God gave the same exact gift to them as to us when we believed in the Master Jesus Christ, how could I object to God?" Hearing it all laid out like that, they quieted down. And then, as it sank in, they started praising God. "It's really happened! God has broken through to the other nations, opened them up to Life!"*

Peter had a success that day. He learned that salvation is not for the few. It wasn't then and it isn't now. God gave the same gift to all, Peter said! I am so glad to be a small part of this celebration, this time of jubilee. Be refreshed tonight, for according to the agenda, the work continues on tomorrow. Peter had a success that day, but the work continued. Be inspired in the morning, at noon, and at midnight; never get tired of doing good. Never get tired of building up people for the Kingdom of God. Never get tired of building justice, building up communities, building a united Church. Then **peace** will come as we do the work of God. We are to walk through His process, trust his strategic provisions, believe that he has a purpose for us, and know that He will give us **peace**. And, with His **peace**, we have blessed assurance of His love.

Love and peace, peace and love—they are united. Love was there at the beginning of time. It was there in God's heart and in His mind. I wasn't there but I am convinced love was there. My Beloved, love is God! **And in God there is His peace—**that peace you have been waiting all your life for arrives in the love of God.

So, people of faith, keep walking, working, witnessing, and kingdom building for God! Where is this "kingdom of God"? Our Savior says in Luke 17:21, "The kingdom of God is within you." God has a plan for each of us and in His plan is His process that has to be walked through, His provisions that must be worked, His purpose that calls for greater witnessing, and His peace He will give us, which is always accompanied by His love.

Stay committed to one another, to fellowship, to share, to experience that harmony, and stay in love. The kind of love that no matter what you have, what you possess, what you are seeking, if you don't have love, you have nothing;

you are nothing. Continue to tell folk that you are affirming, welcoming, and loving.

Yes, there are naysayers, Pharisees, the circumcised of today who say Jesus cannot be in this walk for justice, equality, dignity, inclusivity, peace, and love for all. But the devil is a liar! For God so loved the world… Simply stated He was born to a virgin, walked the earth for 33 years, ministered and taught for 3 years, was persecuted, prosecuted, and crucified, and on the 3rd day the Temple rose, shared 40 more days on the earth teaching and witnessing, and ascended into the heavens because of love.

Beloved **faith walkers**, vessels in this strategic celebration for justice, affirmation, and inclusion of all in the body of Christ, this is not about you. Witnessing for the kingdom of God as a participant through His plan, His process, His provisions, His peace, His love, and His Word is an other-oriented strategy! When it all sinks in, in every city, state, and nation, every family, and every church, we will praise God and say it really happened. God has broken through and opened us **all** up to life and life more abundantly.

The last reported words spoken by Steve Jobs just before he died were, "Oh wow, oh wow, oh wow." I look forward to the day when all those who are against us will say "Oh wow"! That's what the $20 bill, the naysayers, the unbelievers will one day say about the Church of the living God, "Oh wow, oh wow, oh wow!"…

NOTE

1. 1 John 4:4, paraphrased.

EMPOWERMENT AND IDENTITY

Relentless Pursuit

Rosalyn Nichols

BIO. IN BRIEF

Reverend Rosalyn Nichols is a graduate of LeMoyne-Owen College. In 1996, Dr. Nichols graduated summa cum laude from Memphis Theological Seminary and in 2004, she received a Doctor of Ministry degree from Virginia Union University. Dr. Nichols was the first ordained clergywoman to serve as visiting professor at the Gweru Baptist Theological Seminary in Gweru, Zimbabwe, in southern Africa. She has received numerous awards including the Memphis Community Leader Award, the Visionaries Trailblazer Award, and the Henry Logan Starks Alumni Award. She is a lifetime member of the NAACP and a member of Alpha Kappa Alpha Sorority, Inc., Beta Epsilon Omega Chapter.

Judges 1:11-15 (New Living Translation)

From there they marched against the people living in the town of Debir (formerly called Kiriath-sepher). Then Caleb said, "I will give my daughter Acsah in marriage to the one who attacks and captures Kiriath-sepher." Othniel, the son of Caleb's younger brother Kenaz, was the one who conquered it, so Acsah became Othniel's wife. When Acsah

*married Othniel, she urged him to ask her father for an additional field.
As she got down off her donkey, Caleb asked her, "What is it? What can
I do for you?" She said, "Give me a further blessing. You have been kind
enough to give me land in the Negev; please give me springs as well." So
Caleb gave her the upper and lower springs.*

I want you to consider with me the images that are presented to us of women who are business-minded. Think of the adjectives, the nouns, the descriptions given to women who have a mind for business, women who are gifted in matters of business, women who have a keen ability to look ahead, despite the challenges and limitations, disabilities, restrictions, and outright devaluing of themselves. These are women who are able to, in spite of it all, acquire more out of life than is prescribed to them.

Think of the names, the adjectives, the descriptions given to women who are not afraid to deal in business, who do not think it out of place to deal in business and the politics of business, who recognize and own their power in business.

I have a younger cousin. He is a young man now, but when he was a toddler, just learning how to speak, I taught him to say, *I am a good boy. I am a smart boy. And I am cute too.* Whenever I was preaching I would have him stand up and I'd say, RonAlan, tell these people who you are, and without hesitation, he would say, *I'm a good boy. I'm a smart boy. And I'm cute too.*

As time went on, I had someone tell me, "You don't need to teach him that. You'll make him arrogant if you teach him that." My response was, No, I'm not making him arrogant. He is a young black boy in America. I'm planting seeds inside of him because I know he lives in a world that would have him think on a daily basis that he is not good, not smart, and not cute! (He's now handsome.) And so when the world comes against him, I want him to have something on the inside that will help him fight on the outside so that he can claim for himself what and who God has created him to be! I haven't forgotten where I'm going.

There is, I tell you, an assault upon the women in our world who are smart, shrewd, and business-savvy. There is a devious, subversive, destructive attack upon women who know how to handle their business and therefore are able to speak up for themselves and ask for more in life. The definition of entrepreneurship is the relentless pursuit of opportunity beyond resources currently controlled. *Let me say that again.* The definition of entrepreneurship is the relentless pursuit of opportunity beyond resources currently controlled.

There is, I tell you, an assault, an attack, an aggressive campaign underfoot in our country and our world against women who have been created in God's own image and God-ordained to be savvy, smart, shrewd, and business-minded. These are women whom God has gifted with entrepreneurial spirits, with a relentless pursuit of opportunity beyond resources currently controlled. These women are called devils. They are called be-aches. They are called aggressive, and hard to work with. They are referred to as hard, cold, calculating, ruthless, and angry. This is nothing new, but since it is the 21st century, with slavery, suffrage and civil rights now woven into the fabric of our history, with women having fought for the right to be, to vote, to have a voice in the direction of their lives, it is hard to believe that there is still such an aggressive assault upon the image of women who can make their own way.

Despite the advancement of women into places and spaces of prestige and position, there is a backlash against the woman who is business-minded, who is business-savvy, who has an acumen for finance and a gift for the art of the deal. Now the message that young women are receiving is a consistent message that it is impossible to be a woman who is both shrewd, smart, and savvy and in a healthy, loving, and supportive relationship. She will have to give up something to get to the top in business. And because the highest good for any woman, we assume, is a relationship with a man, that means there is only one choice for a woman to make.

From the movie *Something New* to *Deliver Us from Eva* to *The Devil Wears Prada*, the message is clear—a shrewd, savvy, smart, ambitious business-minded woman is a devil to be avoided. A woman who is smart, creative, and forward-thinking is a devil who has no personal life, who cannot keep a husband, whose children don't know her name, and who is lonely and sad in the end.

From Martha Stewart to Ursula Burns (the sister who heads Xerox), the expectation is that a woman who is gifted for business is destined to be alone; and conversely therefore a woman should settle and accept the limitations placed upon her and want no more.

A radio DJ interviewing singer Keisha Cole several years ago asked her about rumors that she was hard to work with, a be-ach, a problem. The young woman's response was, *You know, girls are taught to be all nice, but I'm trying to build my business. I can't be nice; I have to handle my business like a man.* A woman who is shrewd, savvy, and has an eye for business runs the risk of believing that she has to give up her femininity. If she is business-minded the world tells this young woman that she must handle her business like a man. Keisha Cole and others like her need an image of womanhood that allows a woman to be business-minded and not feel the need to behave or think like a man in order to succeed in life.

Little girls, when they start school, come in with the same level of competence and confidence in arithmetic and mathematics as boys. But by the time those same girls reach the age of 13 there is an across-the-board marked decline in achievement. Girls, they say, begin to dummy down. There are subtle messages that teach, condition, and train girls away from numbers, from business, from financial matters, from the relentless pursuit of opportunities beyond resources currently controlled.

Young women need to see an image of a woman, a real woman in the relentless pursuit of opportunity beyond resources currently controlled. They need the image of a woman, a real woman, who does not sacrifice the full pleasure and strength of womanhood as she acquires more for herself than life currently has told her she can have. We need to see images of women, real women who see their womanhood as an asset, a prize, a gift that includes good old-fashioned business sense. We need images of women that challenge us against thinking that business is a man's world and that in order to be in it you have to act like a man. Let's get rid of images that say that engaging in business transactions, negotiating, and bartering is what a woman does when she ain't got no man, can't work with a man, and doesn't have time for a man.

I believe women need to be reminded that shrewd and savvy does not mean sad and lonely, nor does it mean you have to become a ride-or-die chick. To be shrewd, savvy, and smart also does not mean that you have to switch around in coochie cutters, blurring the lines, while you twerk your way into a wrecking-ball life.

So, I looked around and I asked the Lord to fashion for us an image of womanhood that is shrewd, smart, connected, respected, and admired. I asked the Lord to fashion for us an image of a woman who did not let the limited expectations of the world she lived in prevent her from living up to and asking for more of life than was given to her. I asked the Lord to fashion for us a woman in the relentless pursuit of opportunity beyond the resources currently controlled.

I asked the Lord and the Lord introduced me to a woman named Acsah!

Acsah—her name means ornamental bracelet, anklet, and trinket. And that's just how she was treated in her world. A woman born into a sea of politics and war, a woman caught between men and the get-rich-or-die-tryin' games they played. Acsah was treated like the grand prize at the Kentucky Derby, like the big belt in the heavyweight championship, like the big rings guys get for winning the Super Bowl. Acsah was used as a tool for war. Just like those oil fields abroad for which we too often lose our sons and daughters, Acsah was used like bait to lure a fish to the hook.

Caleb, her father, said, *I will give my daughter Acsah in marriage to the man who attacks and captures Debir, Kiriath-sepher.* Like Robert Redford in the movie *Indecent Proposal,* Caleb, caught up in the thirst for the win, offers up his beloved daughter as a reward to the man who would defeat his enemy.

I found it hard to relate to this part of Acsah's story. I asked the Lord, *How can you fashion this woman into the image we need?* I can't get with this woman whose father treated her this way. Even if it was just the culture of her day, I can't redeem this portion of Acsah's story. I can't somehow make this okay or justified.

But thanks be to God, God did not say I had to, after all. Some things that happen to us cannot be, nor should they be, made okay. They will not get better by and by. Some stuff will not turn into your higher good, a ministry, or a testimony. Some things in life are just garbage that you have to throw out, like bad files on your computer that you just have to delete.

The reality of Acsah's life could not be made okay simply because her father was otherwise a good man. He still used her for his own benefit. Even if it was a cultural thing, that still doesn't make it good. Misogyny, hating on women in hip-hop music, may be culturally what's done, but it ain't good. Paying women less than men for the same work may be what's done, but it ain't good. Refusing to accept women as pastors may be what is often done, but it ain't good. Using your daughter as a tool to get what you want may be culturally acceptable, but, Caleb, it ain't ok!

And if we're not careful, we might just miss hearing Acsah's story because of this reality in her life. But God would not have us simply dismiss Acsah's life because it is wrapped up in some bad packaging. Acsah has a blessing for someone today. There is someone here today whom life has wrapped in some jacked-up packaging, and there is some stuff that has happened to you in your life that ain't okay, and can't just simply be made right. But in the midst of it, don't think there is not value in your story. Don't think God has left you without purpose to your story. Don't think God ain't working things out for your good in spite of your story!

Acsah has a message in the midst of the mess of her story. Acsah is everyone who lives on the margins of life, on the fringes, who often is overlooked and discounted in life.

But sometimes it's by looking at the person on the fringes, that person you're just about to overlook, that you learn what you really need to know about life. I learned that from Jesus!

Acsah makes us tilt our heads a bit to look at her more closely. Acsah makes us glance around, look between the lines. Acsah makes us blink so we can focus in a bit more. She makes us stop and take notice. Here she is, little old Acsah, a virgin, a daughter, eye candy, a door prize. Acsah is in the middle between her father willing to give her away and the man willing to fight for her. Acsah is caught between a community at war and the promise of new life. Acsah is caught between a culture that expected women to be seen and not heard. She is treated like property and is given away without so much as a question.

We are introduced to Acsah without her saying a word. But when she opens her mouth, we discover a woman who does not let all the garbage going on around her keep her from getting what was best for Acsah! Acsah had the deck stacked against her—war, politics, sexism, the thirst for power, competition, male ego, and pride—but Acsah did not let any of that blind her, nor convince her that she had no voice, no say, and no role to play in her own life.

Jane Gates, great, great grandmother of African American history professor Dr. Henry Louis Gates, was born into slavery, was farmed out, rented, and passed on like furniture in the will when her slave owners died. But Jane Gates was shrewd, smart, and had a keen eye for business. Within a few short years into her freedom in 1874, she took $1,400 in cold hard cash and this former slave purchased for herself a two-story home that still stands today! Jane Gates had the spirit of Acsah! The spirit of Acsah does not give up or give in!

The Bible says that Acsah urged Othniel to get more than just her. Her father had promised to give him a wife. Because of Acsah, Othniel was able to get land as well. One writer says that in the politics of war, Acsah represented for Othniel more than just a wife; she represented relationships, connections, and a network. Othniel was not simply gaining a wife, but the marriage represented for Othniel greater influence and greater opportunity. Acsah brought to the table with Othniel the possibility of greater rewards. In ancient Israel, as is true today, two things are of pivotal value: family ties and land. The rewards of loyal service back then were land and a woman. Othniel was given the woman, but it was because of the woman that he was able to acquire the land.

Some of us would do well to remember that marriage, for all of its love and romance, is also political. It is also social. It is also a business transaction. Marriage is an enterprise, and the business in the enterprise of marriage is the building of a life together. Some of us get so caught up in the fantasy, the romance, how she or he makes us feel, we lose focus. We neglect to consider that when the light bill is due, the only *feeling* that matters is the *feeling* of satisfaction that the bill is paid! Acsah teaches us, reminds us, and cautions us not to be so overwhelmed by the notion of becoming someone's spouse that we lose sight of the big picture, the business of marriage.

Acsah understood this, and for this reason she encouraged her husband to acquire some land. Some people may call Acsah bossy; some may call her pushy, not very ladylike, or not a good submissive wife. I believe God created Acsah as shrewd, savvy, smart, and beautiful too!

I know she was cute! Men were willing to put their lives on the line in war, to kill or be killed to get the chance to end up with her as their bride. You don't put your life on the line for a scrub. This woman had it all, she was the real deal. With Acsah by his side, he could become the President! That's the spirit of Acsah!

She wasn't so concerned with the wedding day that she missed what they would have after the cake had been eaten and the bouquet had been tossed. Her mind wasn't on how long her veil would be or how many bridesmaids she would have. She wasn't interested in being a bridezilla. Acsah understood that all of that was temporary but what was lasting was land. What they could build a life upon was land. What they'd be able to live on was not the pictures from the wedding, but land! Othniel got the woman and the woman got the land.

How much further along would we be as a people if we cared more about things of value than impressing people with our meaningless things? Flossing and glossing with lint in our pockets and bill collectors knocking at our door! Acsah was not a gold digger, but she wasn't planning on being with no broke, broke…!

Acsah was a shrewd, smart, savvy woman. She was a woman in the relentless pursuit of opportunity beyond resources currently controlled. In a world where men were killing and fighting over promised land, Acsah wanted her father to promise to give her some land.

Olive Ann Beech married Walter Beech. He had been a World War I flying ace. When the war was over, he was a barnstormer. I have no clue what either of those is, but I do know that together Ann and Walter founded Beech Aircraft Corporation. Walter loved the engineering and designing of aircrafts, but he didn't know or feel comfortable doing the business of the company. Ann, on the other hand, was a business genius. She was shrewd, savvy, and smart, and together they were able to build an empire!

In the 1950s, Flora Cole Cochran along with her husband, Socrates Cochran, opened Flora's Flower Shop, the first black-female-owned flower shop in Memphis, Tennessee. Racist white wholesale shops did not deter her; limited resources did not deter her; limited education and no degree did not deter her. Not only did she have a love for flowers, but also she had a mind for business and became the premiere flower shop in the city for well over 40 years. That is the spirit of Acsah!

Chinese Emperor Huang Di gets the credit for raising silk, but it was his wife Lei-Tzu who discovered silk and turned it into a fabric that would change the way women and men dressed around the world. The spirit of Acsah reminds us that it is appropriate for a woman to have a mind for business and to have a gift for transacting business.

But this is not only a message about a shrewd, savvy, smart businesswoman. This is not only a message about women overcoming the odds and handling their business. What led me to Acsah was not that she got her father to give her some land. No, in fact it was what happened *after* she got the land that really let me know that Acsah was the woman God had fashioned for us as the image we need today. It was what Acsah did after she got the land, after she got off that donkey, that caught my eye and drew me to want to get to know more about this woman of God.

The Word says, as she got down off her donkey, Caleb asked her, "What is it? What can I do for you?" She said, "Give me a further blessing. You have been kind enough to give me land in the Negev; please give me springs as well." So Caleb gave her the upper and lower springs.

Acsah said, give me a further blessing. I like Acsah not just because she was assertive. I like Acsah not just because she was politically astute. I like Acsah not just because she knew how to work the system. I like Acsah because she was a woman in the relentless pursuit of opportunities beyond resources currently controlled.

I like Acsah because she wasn't afraid to ask for more! She was not afraid to believe in the possibility that life had more to offer her. She was a woman with enough faith to believe in a God who could do exceedingly abundantly more than she could think or ask! I tell you I believe what we need today is not more women who want more for the sake of having more, but instead we need women of faith who believe more is available when we walk by faith and not by sight.

The word says that Acsah asked her father for a further blessing. And what I really like is that she knew what that further blessing was that she wanted. Acsah knew what the right more was. Othniel got the land and that was good, but what good is land in the desert without water to care for it? Acsah asked for the water that they would need to care for the land.

Acsah didn't just ask for a well; she asked for the source for every well. That way not only would she have water for her own land, but she also would operate the water company in her area and have not just water but also a revenue stream! We can shout right there.

That's why I love Acsah. I love a smart, savvy, shrewd woman in the relentless pursuit of opportunities beyond resources currently controlled!

Acsah is the woman who knows how to not just buy the house, but also the duplex and rent out two of the rooms. Acsah is the woman who is more interested in Apple stock than owning an Apple gadget. She is a woman who wants her money to work for her more than her always working for money. She is a woman who knows that the man in her life must add value to her life, and not simply be a trinket so that she can say she has a man in her life.

Acsah knew how to ask, what to ask for, and who to ask. She asked her father! She knew her father loved her. She knew her father would give her what she asked for. She knew her father would give her more!

If Acsah knew her father, Caleb, would give her more, I need some daughters of the Most High to know God wants more for you. I hear God saying, What is it? What can I do for you?

God wants to give you more! God has everything you need—"pressed down, shaken together and running over." Be bold like Acsah, be relentless, and ask God for more—the right more.

Change the Atmosphere

Sharon Riley

BIO. IN BRIEF

Pastor Sharon Riley earned a Bachelor of Science from the
University of Florida in Gainesville, Florida, and an Honorary
Doctorate of Divinity Degree from the St. Thomas Christian
College in Jacksonville, Florida. She currently serves as
the Senior Pastor of Agape Perfecting Praise and Worship
Center, where she has served faithfully for 15 years.
Pastor Riley also facilitates radio broadcasts, where she can be
heard ministering throughout the Central Florida region.
Her sermons have appeared in *The Orland Times Weekly*
and central Florida's *GOSPELNOW Christian Lifestyle
Magazine*, of which she serves as the managing editor.

Genesis 41:33-41 (New Living Translation)
*"Therefore, Pharaoh should find an intelligent and wise man and put
him in charge of the entire land of Egypt. Then Pharaoh should appoint
supervisors over the land and let them collect one-fifth of all the crops
during the seven good years. Have them gather all the food produced in
the good years that are just ahead and bring it to Pharaoh's storehouses.
Store it away, and guard it so there will be food in the cities. That way*

there will be enough to eat when the seven years of famine come to the land of Egypt. Otherwise this famine will destroy the land."

Joseph's suggestions were well received by Pharaoh and his officials. So Pharaoh asked his officials, "Can we find anyone else like this man so obviously filled with the spirit of God?" Then Pharaoh said to Joseph, "Since God has revealed the meaning of the dreams to you, clearly no one else is as intelligent or wise as you are. You will be in charge of my court, and all my people will take orders from you. Only I, sitting on my throne, will have a rank higher than yours."

Pharaoh said to Joseph, "I hereby put you in charge of the entire land of Egypt."

It was the fourth quarter. 5.2 seconds remained. The score was tied at 95, and the period that typically represents the end of regulation play turned into overtime for the Miami Heat and the San Antonio Spurs in Game 6 of the 2013 NBA Playoffs. The two teams exerted comparable effort against one another, as they both demonstrated exceptional mastery of the game. What happened in the final overtime period of game six was the game-changer, forcing a seventh challenge and creating another opportunity for the Miami Heat to contend for the NBA Championship.

What do you do in the space of time you have been given, how do you handle the opportunities afforded you, and where you are positioned at a particular moment? Your response to these questions ultimately determines the character of your season, the condition of the atmosphere around you, and your outcomes. If you don't like the way things are going, change them. Take full advantage of the time, opportunity, and position in which you find yourself. **Change your atmosphere!**

The events in Game 6 of the 2013 NBA finals caused some to develop a premature assumption about the game's outcome, as the San Antonio Spurs appeared to have the advantage. But, at the last minute, the Miami Heat changed the atmosphere. The cheers of Spurs fans were soon drowned out by the roar of Heat fans as the late change in the fourth period turned the tables in favor of the Miami Heat, sending the game into overtime.

In the NBA, there are four 12-minute periods in regulation play, with overtime being an additional period of play specified under the rules to bring a game to a decision and avoid declaring the game a tie. The only reason that overtime becomes necessary is because no one has prevailed as the clear winner at the end of regulation time. There are 5-minute overtime periods until someone wins. The extra period presents additional opportunities for the advantage to be taken by one and lost by another. Someone must emerge the victor. Someone must make and execute decisions that support a favorable outcome for them; someone must maximize the moment.

Joseph of the Bible, like the Miami Heat, rose to prominence through a series of game-changing events. His responses to the circumstances confronting him paved his path to greatness. He survived the scorn of his siblings, rejected the seductions of the wife of one of his employers, and stayed strong and sane through a thirteen-year prison sentence that he served for a crime he did not commit! I can only imagine Joseph thinking that if he had never gone to check on his brothers that day he would never have landed in that pit, never been put on the slave market, never met Potiphar's wife, and certainly never ended up in prison.

As unsettling as these events were for Joseph, each of them helped get him to his ultimate position in the pharaoh's palace. These right-place right-time encounters for Joseph worked in succession to position him to become Egypt's atmosphere-changer and a savior for Israel. When events occur contrary to the way we would have ordered or designed them, it is sometimes difficult for us to recognize that the uncomfortable places and grave misfortunes are part of God's plan to position us as atmosphere-changers later. **Atmosphere-changers are always in the right place at the right time even if they do not know it.**

Our most common understanding of time is based on the ancient Greek word *chronos*, referring to chronological or sequential time, like that we see on clocks and calendars. The ancient Greeks had another word for time, *kairos*, meaning the right or opportune moment (the supreme moment), a moment of indeterminate time in which something special happens. While *chronos* is quantitative, *kairos* is qualitative, pointing to the nature of something. *Kairos* refers to "a passing instance when an opening appears which must be driven through with force if success is to be achieved."[1] *Kairos* supports the fact that there exists an opportunity to change the atmosphere.

The Ancient Greek philosopher Aristotle viewed *kairos* as the "context of space and time in which proof is delivered."[2] This is precisely what happened for the Miami Heat. They literally drove through an opening with uncontestable force, and delivered the proof that they were the better managers of the circumstances presented. It was their accurate judgment while maximizing their moments that allowed them to change the atmosphere around them. The Miami Heat could have given up in the fourth period of Game 6 when they were behind on the scoreboard, but the game wasn't over. Recognizing that there was still time on the clock, they played to gain more playing time.

In our frustrations resulting from the fickle nature of life, the temptation looms to quit the game prematurely. But the game "ain't" over if you send it into overtime. The Miami Heat made it beyond regulation play into multiple overtime periods. It would have been foolish of them to get close to winning the game and decide to throw in the towel. As a matter of fact, they didn't have a towel to throw in. Towels don't go into the game; they remain on the bench and on the sidelines of the court. Towel-toting players are only on the bench, not in the game!

You cannot afford to spend your life on the bench. Put down your towel and quit trying to quit. You are an atmosphere-changer; get in the game and stay in the game. Come out of the locker room, get off the bench, put that towel down; the clock is still ticking. Until the clock runs out, you still have time. Shift your thinking, your behavior, and your focus. Change your atmosphere!

Joseph was no towel-toten' bench warmer. The envy and rejection of his brothers could have prevented his palace experience, if he were anybody else; but he was Joseph, Jacob's eleventh son and Rachel's first. He was Joseph, whose name means "God will add or increase." The status associated with his name defied the condescending and cruel manner in which his brothers dealt with him. Their maltreatment of the dreamer was designed to decrease him; but how in the world can you decrease someone whose name means "God will increase"? Your own folk may seek to minimize you, but God has marked you for greatness, so don't waste time on haters. **Atmosphere-changers are resilient.**

How many times have we made a decision to abandon something based on someone else's perception of us? How many ministry opportunities have we missed because of how we felt in response to someone's behavior toward us? How many dreams have we deferred for fear we would be rejected? How many times has the Lord sent us to check on our brothers, and we refused the assignment because those same brothers previously mistreated us? If you are going to be an atmosphere-changer, pull yourself together, and start maximizing your moments. Toughen up. Get back on your knees and ask God to help you remain resilient and emotionally healthy. The game isn't over. Are you **resilient** enough to stay in the game?

Joseph could have benched himself after the favor of his father served to isolate him from members of the family. But, benching himself would have meant decrease and not increase. He could have thrown in the towel after his dreams caused his brothers to hate him even more; but that would have contradicted the status God had given him. Increase means to make greater, multiply, or reproduce; and when God is the mastermind behind the growth, who can curse it, kill it, or confine it? No one!

Since the clock is still ticking, *chronos* and *kairos* are on your side. You have moments and appointments remaining in your favor. In the New Testament, *kairos* means the appointed time in the purpose of God, the time when God displays decisive action.[3] It's God's movement that positions you to shift the atmosphere. It's God's orchestration along with your participation that can produce an unprecedented, unparalleled manifestation of achievement in your life, your home, your business, and your ministry. It's God's movement, pushing you to make a move that will shift something in the larger scheme of things in your life. Joseph did not place himself in the pit, Potiphar's house, the prison, or the palace. God did! But Joseph's response to each of these situations was correct and consistent with his godly character. It was Potiphar's wife failure to make Joseph unethical that fostered her false accusation against Joseph. Her call for him to contradict his convictions and compromise his character went unheeded. The best response he knew to offer was to run. Just as atmosphere-changers are in the right place at the right time, and they are resilient, **atmosphere-changers also respond correctly**!

Within chronological, sequential time, we are each afforded *kairos* moments. How we respond in those moments determines what happens in the next season of our life. We can either shift our atmosphere for the better, or shut it down, based upon how we respond to God's movement. The Hebrew perspective on time and seasons teaches that life is filled with moments when certain actions and responses are called for or required. These moments do not arrive pre-packaged with a bow, with us as passive observers, absolved of responsibility. Instead, these are the occasions when a right response is required. Life isn't set before you get here. Your responses, your choices, your actions—and the actions of all of the rest of the created order—shape what happens next.

The traffic accident occurs because someone made a decision, or offered a response to some behavior or action of another. The collision resulted from the impact of two or more contradictory responses at a single moment in time. The argument only develops because of the reply or reaction given at a particular time. The promotion generally comes because of consistent right responses and behaviors over time.

What you do in your moments not only has temporal, sometimes immediate effects, but also has *eternal consequences*. When you responded to the invitation to receive Christ as your personal Savior, you offered a "right" response that carries an eternal benefit. When you decided to remain upset with the one who offended you, instead of forgiving them, you offered a wrong response that carries with it eternal consequences. This posture of unforgiveness also carries with it far-reaching implications that may negatively affect future relationships. Decisions you made about when to have children and how to care for them financially and emotionally have immediate consequences and eternal consequences. What you do in one season has major implications on the next.

Chaos theory is a mathematical field of study applicable to disciplines such as engineering, economics, physics, biology, and philosophy. It concentrates on the behavior of dynamic systems that are highly sensitive to initial conditions. Well, in chaos theory there is a concept known as the butterfly effect. In chaos theory, the butterfly effect refers to the sensitive dependency on initial conditions in which a small change at one place in a deterministic *nonlinear system* can result in large differences in a later state. In essence, the present can determine the future.

The butterfly effect may apply in the physical or natural realm, but you can't always apply it in the spiritual realm. In the spiritual realm, when God's grace is applied, the butterfly effect flies right out the window. Just ask the woman caught in the act of adultery; this was her initial condition. The grace of the Savior released her from a sentence of death into a life of forgiveness and freedom. Just ask Paul who was adamant about stopping Jesus believers, even holding the coat of the man who stoned the apostle Stephen; this was his initial condition. Then the grace of God threw him from the beast he was riding and set him on the road to being the greatest church builder Christianity has ever known. Just ask any believer you know.

We can all tell you that we were on our way to hell and living lives with poor purposes. But the grace of God picked us up, turned us around, and placed our feet on solid ground! But in every instance, when grace was applied, a "yes" of acceptance was required. **Atmosphere-changers must respond correctly.** One small change in their initial condition can result in major shifts in the atmosphere at a later time.

Next, the text reminds us that Pharaoh was advised by Joseph to "select a discerning and wise man, and set him over the land of Egypt." Pharaoh was responsible for choosing the best, most suitable, most competent man for the job. Only the most discerning man with wisdom and management proficiency would do. In order to choose a man of this caliber, Pharaoh had to possess the ability to recognize a man of this caliber. Joseph's brothers lacked the ability to recognize the greatness in their midst because they were too preoccupied with minimizing him because he held the favor of his father. Push past the seasons when you are passed over for promotion and recognition; not everyone is qualified to recognize greatness. Besides, you have the favor of your Father.

Joseph went from avoiding the seductions of Potiphar's wife and managing the state of affairs in Potiphar's house, being a dream interpreter in prison, to advising Pharaoh on the future economic state of Egypt. Atmosphere-changers can never be confined to a circle when God has called them to the nation. The clique that you are determined to be a member of is too small for the greatness in you. The circle of Joseph's immediate family, the pit, the prestigious management position in Potiphar's house, and the prison were confines from which Joseph would be thrown out, pulled out, driven out, and called out. The impact of an atmosphere-changer is frustrating in small places, but effective and revolutionary in the place to which they are called to change the atmosphere. But they have to respond correctly.

Let me briefly also point out that **atmosphere-changers are also strategists**. Joseph provided Pharaoh with a strategy to survive the season of famine coming to Egypt. The text states that not only will a governor be necessary, but also "officers over the land, to collect one-fifth of the produce of the land of Egypt." Atmosphere-changers are strategists. They bring a game-changing skill-set to determine the best way to achieve success. Joseph produced a strategy requiring overseers to collect and save 20% of the produce throughout the land of Egypt each year during the seven years of plenty. Atmosphere-changers maximize moments by preparing for the next opportunity. When preparation and opportunity meet, the season shifts. What are you doing to shift your season and change your atmosphere?

Joseph established reserves to sustain Egypt in the time of famine. The purpose for the strategizing and saving was so "the land may not perish during the famine." Joseph was strategizing to survive. By now, Joseph is skilled in carrying on despite trauma or hardship. Since his teen years, Joseph had to persevere. He had to overcome one obstacle after another. He had to keep it moving; he strategized ways to survive and thrive.

Had Joseph not developed strategies to survive as a teenager, in his 20s, and in his 30s, he would not have been a candidate to change the atmosphere later. Atmosphere-changers are not whiners, grumblers, and complainers. They are decisive and flexible. They learn to go with the flow, for it is the small changes made during your initial condition that translate into big differences later. When they won't allow you in the game, get a strategy to change the atmosphere and the game!

Then Pharaoh and his servants considered Joseph's counsel to be wise, and they acknowledged that he was empowered by God. Seeing the benefit of his guidance, Pharaoh deemed Joseph to be the most likely to help Egypt succeed, even when personal success was not Joseph's focus. **Atmosphere-changers are selfless when they could be selfish.** Considering everything Joseph encountered on his way to the palace, he could have forgotten the ones who dissed and dismissed him. He could have ignored the plight of those who wished him dead. Joseph's strategy was to sustain Egypt, and because of Joseph unselfishly seeking the best for a land that was not his own, God providentially sustained nations beyond Egypt's borders, including the land where Joseph's family lived.

It was Joseph's unselfishness that conditioned him to serve. He served his father by checking on his brothers; he served his brothers by looking out for their welfare; he served Potiphar by managing his affairs; he served the warden of the prison; he served Pharaoh and the families of Egypt and those abroad.

If you are going to change the atmosphere, you must find someone to serve other than yourself. I know, our culture conditions us for self-centeredness and self-service, but atmosphere-changers don't mind being counter-cultural. Jesus came to serve, and not to be served; who in the world is greater than He? We have grown accustomed to being accommodated and catered to. But never forget that we are who we are by God's grace. It is the granting of *HIS* wisdom to us that causes us to excel and shine. It is our display of *HIS* gifts that causes others to celebrate us. It is the manifestation of *HIS* power that promotes us. We are tools God uses to bless others. Your atmosphere will change when you are committed to changing someone else's.

A small change to the initial condition of a life that his brothers deemed insignificant resulted in an enormous difference for Joseph, his family, the Egyptians, and bordering nations later. When Rachel named her son Joseph, "God will increase," her idea was limited to her personal hope for another son. God did honor her request with the birth of Benjamin; but God also did exceedingly abundantly above all she could ask or think. Who would have thought that her baby boy, hated by his brothers, would be hailed by the king of Egypt, and save the family from starvation?

Pharaoh asked the question, "Can we find such a one as this, a man in whom is the Spirit of God?" Now the Egyptians didn't believe in Joseph's God, but even to non-believers it was clear that Joseph's gifts came from a divine source. The Bible declares, "The LORD was with Joseph, and he was a successful man" (Genesis 39:2). My last point this morning is that **atmosphere-changers are successful because God guides their success**. The ultimate atmosphere-changer was in Joseph's corner. Everything that Joseph survived he survived because of God. Everything Joseph accomplished he accomplished because of God. The greatness in Joseph came from God. Joseph's outcome was always successful. Joseph always managed to get out of the pits he encountered. He may have been abandoned by his brothers in the pit, but God never left him. In Potiphar's house, God was with him. In prison, God was with him. In Pharaoh's palace, God was with him. The Lord made Joseph prosper in everything he did. Atmosphere-changers are successful because they have God! Even when it appears that they are the underdog, God always shifts the season and the circumstances so that in the end the atmosphere-changer wins.

In the eyes of some, it may have appeared that God was absent, asleep, or just not paying attention to Joseph. But for every injustice Joseph suffered, God rewarded him. Being sold into slavery, sexually harassed, and sentenced unjustly were merely setbacks that allowed Joseph to make a greater difference later. The Bible reminds us that our light affliction is temporary, and it is working for us a far more exceeding eternal weight of glory.[4] Affliction never seems light or temporary when you are in the middle of it. Thrown into a pit and not knowing his fate, Joseph most likely saw each predicament as heavy and eternal, not light and temporary. The permanence of the slave trade and the prison bars must have screamed to him, "This is it, Joseph!" But God was with him. An atmosphere-changer's life is always wrapped in the purposes of God, and God's purposes always prevail!

For Joseph, for Egypt, but more importantly for Israel, God's purposes prevailed. For the preservation of his family and his people, God used Joseph to change the atmosphere around him. The reason you were called off of the bench and into the game, and the reason you have been selected to survive every disappointing, isolating, traumatizing experience in your life and enabled to come out with a strategy for success, is because God put you in the right place at the right time to change the atmosphere. The strategy that God has given you isn't just about you. It's about your family becoming greater, your company becoming more prosperous, your community becoming stronger, and your life bringing more glory to God. So go ahead and change the atmosphere! Change it! Change it! Turn it upside down and right side up! Change it.

NOTES

1. James Strong, *Strong's Greek Dictionary of the Bible* (Kindle, 2011).

2. Eric Charles White, *Kaironomia: On the Will-to-Invent* (Ithaca, NY: Cornell University Press, 1987), 13.

3. Ibid.

4. 2 Corinthians 4:17.

Fight the Power

Lisa D. Jenkins

BIO. IN BRIEF

Reverend Lisa D. Jenkins is the Pastor of St. Matthew's
Baptist Church in Harlem, New York. She received
her BA in Communications from Pace University and her
M.Div. from New York Theological Seminary. She is the
founder of El DiJae Ministries, a personal and community
empowerment non-profit. Lisa has taught New Testament
Studies and Biblical Exegesis at New York Theological
Seminary and serves as an adjunct professor teaching
Cultural Diversity in the History and Philosophy
Department at York College/City University of New York.
She is the first female to serve in the Pastor's Division
of the Empire Baptist Missionary Convention and is a
member of Delta Sigma Theta Sorority, Inc.

Mark 5:1-15 (New Revised Standard Version)

*They came to the other side of the sea, to the country of the Gerasenes.
And when he had stepped out of the boat, immediately a man out of the
tombs with an unclean spirit met him. He lived among the tombs; and
no one could restrain him anymore, even with a chain; for he had often
been restrained with shackles and chains, but the chains he wrenched*

apart, and the shackles he broke in pieces; and no one had the strength to subdue him. Night and day among the tombs and on the mountains he was always howling and bruising himself with stones. When he saw Jesus from a distance, he ran and bowed down before him; and he shouted at the top of his voice, "What have you to do with me, Jesus, Son of the Most High God? I adjure you by God, do not torment me." For he had said to him, "Come out of the man, you unclean spirit!" Then Jesus asked him, "What is your name?" He replied, "My name is Legion; for we are many." He begged him earnestly not to send them out of the country. Now there on the hillside a great herd of swine was feeding; and the unclean spirits begged him, "Send us into the swine; let us enter them." So he gave them permission. And the unclean spirits came out and entered the swine; and the herd, numbering about two thousand, rushed down the steep bank into the sea, and were drowned in the sea.

The swineherds ran off and told it in the city and in the country. Then people came to see what it was that had happened. They came to Jesus and saw the demoniac sitting there, clothed and in his right mind, the very man who had had the legion; and they were afraid.

I remember when my son was 12 or 13 we had a dialogue about hip-hop music. I was telling Jordan what I believed real hip-hop music was. And although he didn't believe me at the time, I told him that my generation invented hip-hop. And because I was around when hip-hop was born, I know that hip-hop was not intended to be laced with vulgarity and filth. It was not born to profit from negativity in black culture. It was not born for the exploitation and consumerization of the bodies of our young sisters. Hip-hop was born to raise the consciousness of a community; to wake up folk who were sleeping; to activate the inactive. Hip-hop was designed to blast people into reality. And so, I'm constantly telling my son that what he hears on the airwaves today is most often not real hip-hop. It's noise made by those who are ripping off the genre. It's rhymes and rhythms made by individuals who have very little insight. The messages of much of what many today call hip-hop leave much to be desired. No longer do hip-hop artists use this musical art form to do political protesting and to fight for social justice.

So imagine my surprise when I inadvertently find out that Jordan had burned a CD of old school hip-hop. He had Run DMC, Africa Bambata, De La Soul, but most importantly, Jordan heard Public Enemy! Back in 1989, Chuck D, Professor Griff, and Flavor Flav (collectively known as Public Enemy) released the album *Fear of a Black Planet,* which included the hit song "Fight the Power." "Fight the Power" forcefully declared, *"Gotta give us what we need, give us what we want; freedom of speech, freedom or death, got to fight the powers that be."* Public Enemy realized that there were powers that were holding black people down in a death cycle of poverty, homelessness, and illiteracy. Public Enemy also realized that ignorance was a destructive tool.

And because of the enemy, because of this power that has snaked its way into our community, there is a destructive force working on the inside of so many, making its way to the outside seeking to destroy the entire body, both of individuals and the village.

What is it that keeps an individual confined, incarcerated—mentally and physically? What keeps a people down, fearful, afraid, believing there's no ability to break out and break through? What is it that brainwashes one to believe that a mind is not really a terrible thing to waste?

Well, let's take a look at a brother from the hood for some answers. In this passage we have the story of the Gerasene Demoniac. This is a man possessed by a demon. And the Bible says that this demon-possessed man lived among the tombs. Jewish ritual practices of the time separated the world into clean and unclean; the tombs or the graveyard was an unclean place.

I like Mark's version because through it we can really deal with some dirty stuff. So we deal right from the start with the fact that this man lived among that which was unclean—that which was dead, dormant, and lifeless. He made that which was barren of life his home, where he abided, where he stayed. The place that was void of life and activity was his crib. That was the place he laid his head every night. Think about living life among the dead.

There are some folk here today who are living their lives among the dead—dead-end situations. They are going about day-to-day business in graves of despair. Dead-end jobs, dead-end-relationships, dead-end entanglements that have them going out of their mind, going crazy. But there is good news!

Despite the tragic nature of this story, it's really a good news story. It's a good news story because it begins with a visit from Jesus. Verse 1 says that Jesus and his disciples "**went across the lake** to the region of the Gerasenes," where this demon-possessed man lived. This is important because it says Jesus and his disciples went *across,* and if you look at a map of this region, you will see that Jesus goes from the west side of the lake where the Jews live to the east side where the Gentiles live. The west side is where the holy folk lived, the bougie folk, the folk who can do no wrong. Jesus leaves that side and he crosses over to the east side, where the Gentiles live—the unholy folk, the people nobody wants to deal with. Gentiles were people on the wrong side of the tracks. But Jesus crosses over the boundaries to get to people nobody wanted to deal with. Jesus crosses the tracks, the Sea of Galilee, to get with the regular folk. And I like that about Jesus. Jesus wants to get with the regular folk. But even more than that, I love it that Jesus weathers a storm to get to this man.

Chapter 4 has already told us that Jesus has finished preaching by the lake, and he and his boys get in a boat. A Storm creeps up on 'em, but Jesus is not worried, 'cause he's focused on the work he's got to do. Jesus goes through a storm, gets tired of it, and says, "Look, peace, be still." Jesus stopped a storm in its tracks to get to this man.

And that's what Jesus does to get to you. Jesus *goes* through whatever is necessary to get *to* you. From the beginning of time, Jesus has been trying to get to you. Jesus came down from heaven to get TO you, to get WITH you, to save you, and to deliver you. I won't dwell on what I may be going through. Not when I think about Jesus and what he's done, what he's endured, what he's been through, all because he loved me enough to get to me, cherished me enough to be with me, and had enough mercy on me to deliver me!

So Jesus crosses the Sea of Galilee to the other side of the tracks where the Gentiles are. The Gentiles are like the folk in the caste systems in India known as the Untouchables. Jesus weathered a storm so that he could cross the tracks and touch the untouchables, heal the sick, save the lost, give the blind their sight, give the deaf their hearing, and the lame the ability to walk, to deliver the downtrodden, and exorcise some demons.

And can I just pause there, 'cause we need to understand that too often in this country people of color are treated as untouchable! I know we have a Black president, and I believed he would be re-elected. BUT, if you just look at the television, open a newspaper, check out social media, you will see that STILL all too often, we are bombarded by individuals who have no problem spewing their bigoted beliefs simply because there are now folks in leadership who do not look like they do. But Jesus cuts through the racism and injustice to reach us right where we are and to give us exactly what we need.

Jesus is in the city to heal the sick since there are many among us who need a healing touch. Jesus comes by West 140th, Jesus walks up and down Amsterdam, finds his way to Lenox Avenue, and even reaches Harlem to find and save the lost. Jesus takes the "A" train to open your eyes to see his blessings, and to open your ears to hear the word of God. Jesus is here right now to pick you up if you're down, to show you the right way to walk. But Jesus is ALSO here to exorcise the demons that are around you. Jesus is still crossing over to see about you and me. I don't care where you are, where you live or reside…Jesus comes to you, to get with you, to give you deliverance, to give you hope, to give you purpose and victory!

So Jesus leaves the holy folk, the church folk, crosses over to the other side, and the first person he meets is a man possessed by demons. I would like to propose, my sisters and brothers, that this man is a representation of the Black Community. What do you mean? I mean the Bible clearly tells us from the beginning that this man lived in the tombs. The tombs were the most undesirable place anyone could live. Even the average Gentile did not live among the tombs. But this man lived in the most undesirable location. He was redlined into an undesirable locale because of who he was. He was a product of societal gerrymandering, relegating him to the tombs. I don't believe he wanted to be in the tombs. For I'm sure that if a hurricane or flood were to come, when the town would be told to evacuate, privileged folk would pack their donkeys and could get out of town. But, because of who he was and where he was, he would be trapped in a situation that would leave him vulnerable in ways that nobody else would understand.

Yeah, this man was Black America the more I look at him. He was shackled and chained. When I think of shackles and chains, I think about a people stolen from their land, shackled, and chained, held hostage and placed in bondage. But I like verses 3 and 4. The end of verse 3 says that he had been chained, but no one could subdue him; no one could bind him, because he tore the chains apart and broke the shackles on his feet. Isn't that like Black Folk too? We are a people who cannot be subdued. A people who cannot be kept in chains. A people who cannot be kept bound. A people who cannot be contained. A people who, according to Nikki Giovanni, *"cannot be comprehended except by our own permission."* A people who cannot be claimed, but instead have a right to **make** a claim.

There was a power, a force trying to hold this man down. Yeah, this man was Black America alright, because the Bible says that no one was strong enough to subdue him. That meant that he was stronger than anyone who tried to touch him, anyone who tried to keep him down. They relegated him to the tombs, but the fact remained that he was stronger than they were and they knew it, and it bothered them. Don't you know folk who are bothered by your strength, intimidated by your beauty, upset by your intellect, and disturbed because of your genius?

How else do I know that this man is Black America? Night and day, this man would not only cry out but would cut himself with stones. Because of the demons, he tried to harm himself, tried to make himself bleed, tried to damage himself. And I propose that because of the demonic forces—racism, classism, sexism, militarism, and every type of institutionalized *ism* designed for over 400 years to oppress and repress us—we are stoning ourselves, inflicting pain, damaging ourselves.

I further propose that this man was doing to himself what he really wanted to do to the demons. And that's like Black America too. The powers that are supposed to protect us have really demonized us, and as a result, we injure ourselves, hinder ourselves, and hold ourselves back. My son reminded me the other day that it was Tupac Shakur who said, "*Black on black crime is never homicide; black on black crime is suicide.*" That's what black on black crime is, it is suicide, but it is also a fight with a demon within our community. That's what gang violence is. It's a fight with a demon in our community. That's what I'm better than you are because I'm lighter, or better educated, or "I pulled myself up by my bootstraps forget about you" is. It's a fight with a demon in our community. That's what it is when our kids are told that they're acting white because they speak well; it is a fight with a demon in our community. Substance abuse, unconcerned parents, irresponsible sexual activity, these are all fights with demons in our community. Unfortunately, like this man, we focus our violence, our hatred, and our frustrations on each other when it's really a demonic and evil system we should be fighting.

But the good news is Jesus is trying to get to us! Jesus gets out of his boat, here comes the demon-possessed man, and the Bible says Jesus **sees the man**. (How many of you know Jesus is looking at you?) Jesus sees this man—just as he is—he sees the broken and scarred man. And the Bible says the man runs and falls at the feet of Jesus. Jesus asks him, "What is your name?" Jesus knew his name. But sometimes you've got to call folk out. Make 'em identify themselves. Jesus asked, *"What is your name?"* Not only did the spirit inside of the man identify itself, it gave up even more info and said, *"We are many."* It said, *"My name is Legion, because we are many."*

The word legion in biblical times was a military term that defined a Roman army battalion. A legion consisted anywhere from 3,000 to 6,000 soldiers whose primary job was to maintain order in the community. The Roman Empire, which controlled the land and the people, perceived their legions to be a source of keeping the people peaceful. But the people in ancient Palestine regarded Rome and its military legions as oppressive, causing devastation, property damage, poverty, and despair. So what appears to be one demon identifies itself as legion, resulting in the truth being revealed that there are many demons causing devastation and despair.

And then the world wonders why we act the way we do. We act the way we do because we wrestle not against flesh and blood, but against principalities, against powers, against the rulers of darkness of this world, against spiritual wickedness in high places. We act the way we do because we're dealing with demons in our communities!

There are demons in our communities! Don't act as if you can't recognize 'em. As long as we've been living in this country, you ought to know demons when you see them! Demons are not little red men and women with pitchforks, tails, and horns. They are forces working in our communities and our families designed to keep us down and un-empowered. They come in the form of unjust policies; they come in the form of bigoted people pretending to be liberal; they are present in our schools. They are present on our job and throughout this country. Quit conversing with 'em. Quit negotiating with 'em. Quit trying to make policies with 'em. You know they won't change. They believe they have too much to lose. God has given us the revelation; it's time now for a revolution! Any revolutionaries in the house?

That's what Christians are empowered to be. As believers, we are empowered to be revolutionaries. We are empowered to go into the streets and declare war on poverty and war on gun violence. We are empowered to speak life to people who know nothing but death and despair. We are empowered by the Holy Spirit to introduce new ideas and dynamics into the culture. It may not be popular and it may not be easy, but it is necessary. Why? Because we are disciples of Jesus the Christ! Do you think Jesus was popular? He was the word which became flesh and dwelt among us (and we beheld his glory, the glory as of the only begotten of the Father), full of grace and truth. We like grace, but we don't always like truth. If you're going to carry the Banner of Truth, you're going to be a disliked revolutionary because the truth is not always popular! That's why the prophets were not always popular, because they spoke the Truth on behalf of God. They were revolutionaries. And so, yes, we like to deal with grace, we like to deal with favor, we love to talk about mercy and goodness, but start talking the truth and folk will scatter. Start identifying the insanity and calling out folk and circumstances for what they are, that is revolutionary.

Most folk do not want to stir up the pot. Most folk do not want to agitate situations—"Let's just let things be," they say. No, God did not put on flesh just to leave well enough alone. God got with us so that he could identify with our situation, eradicate our low expectations, and bring about our liberation and our restoration! God is not passive, Jesus is not uninvolved, and the Holy Ghost is not on a lunch break! If we are true disciples, like our Savior we've got to be involved and fight the powers!

Look at the scripture again. We see what happens. The Bible says that the demons *begged* Jesus to send them into the pigs and Jesus says, fine, just as long as you leave this man. The demons go into the swine, which are ultimately destroyed. The demons BEG to go into the swine, which were like the graveyard at the beginning of our story; the swine are likewise unclean. This lets us know that even demons know that they cannot reside in a clean environment. When Jesus enters your world and God cleans you up, demons know that they are not welcome! When God cleans you up and dusts you off, the devil has to pack up and find another place to hang out. Because by its nature, the devil cannot dwell inside a vessel that is filled with the Holy Ghost. If you're filled with the Holy Ghost, there's no room for Satan or his buddies. And so when Jesus told the demons to scram, they knew they had to relocate to a similar unclean environment—hence, the pigs.

Look at the scripture again; we see what happens. The demons beg Jesus to send them into the pigs and Jesus says fine, just as long as you leave this man. The demons go into the swine, which are ultimately destroyed. But that's not the end. The Bible says that after the commotion, the people came to see Jesus, and in coming to see Jesus, they see the man who was earlier possessed, now sitting, fully clothed and in his right mind. But the sad part of verse 15 says, "They were afraid." The man was clothed and in his right mind, but the people were afraid. The people were fine when the man was crazy; the people were fine when the man was possessed. The people were fine when he was in a controlled situation. But now that he was clothed and in his right mind, now that he was liberated and freed from his graveyard, they were afraid.

Don't you see the problem? The problem for some folk is there has been a movement of exorcism in our community. We're fighting racism, poverty, powerlessness, and mis-education—we've got a Black president and not everybody's happy. And, although the movement is far from over, we have shown that some of us are **clothed and in our right minds**. And because of this, the powers that be are afraid!

We're clothed and we're in our right minds when we know that although we walk through "the valley of the shadow of death, we don't have to fear evil," because God has been and is with us. We're clothed and in our right minds when we know that a "people perish for lack of knowledge but it is the Lord who giveth wisdom, out of HIS mouth comes knowledge and understanding." We're clothed and in our right minds when we know that "greater is he that is in us, than he that is in this world."

Is there anybody in here clothed and in your right mind? The devil tried to kill you. The devil tried to write you off. He sent his demons to try to destroy you. But because God was on your side, he clothed you in victory, and gave you peace of mind.

Oh, I'm clothed and in my right mind today! I might be in the graveyard some days, but that's all right, because the best place for a resurrection experience is a graveyard! I'm coming out because I've got Jesus. Moving day is coming. Jesus is my mover! He's moving some stuff. He's moving some folk. He's moving some situations. He's pruning me; he's preparing me; he's arranging me; he's re-arranging me. But most of all he's raising me!

And, I'm in my right mind enough to know that I'm not waiting until I get to heaven, because I believe God's got some blessings for us right here on earth. And I'm in my right mind enough to fight any powers that tell me otherwise. I'm in my right mind enough to fight any force that tries to hinder me.

There's a revolution. This revolution will not be televised. The revolution will not be a re-run, my brothers and sisters. This revolution will be live. And Jesus is the Star, Jehovah is the Producer, and the Holy Spirit is the Production Manager!

So walk together, children, don't you get weary. Walk together, children, don't you get tired. Walk together, children, don't you get weary. There's a great camp meeting here, now, today, in this Promised Land!

There Is Power in the Name of Jesus to Break Every Chain

Mary Moore

BIO. IN BRIEF

Reverend Mary Moore, M.Div., was elected pastor of
New Salem Baptist Church, in Memphis, Tennessee, in 1997 as
the second female of a black Baptist Church in Shelby County,
where Rev. C. L. Franklin was former pastor. She retired
from the Pastorate of New Salem Baptist Church in 2010.
In 2011, Rev. Moore became the Executive Pastor at
St. Paul Baptist Church in Memphis, Tennessee, where
Dr. Christopher Davis is the Senior Pastor.

Acts 16:25-31 (New Revised Standard Version)
*About midnight Paul and Silas were praying and singing hymns to
God, and the prisoners were listening to them. Suddenly there was an
earthquake, so violent that the foundations of the prison were shaken;
and immediately all the doors were opened and everyone's chains
were unfastened. When the jailer woke up and saw the prison doors
wide open, he drew his sword and was about to kill himself, since he
supposed that the prisoners had escaped. But Paul shouted in a loud*

voice, "Do not harm yourself, for we are all here." The jailer called for
lights, and rushing in, he fell down trembling before Paul and Silas.
Then he brought them outside and said, "Sirs, what must I do to be
saved?" They answered, "Believe on the Lord Jesus, and you will be
saved, you and your household."

I need to tell you on the front end, this sermon today is not for everybody. It's only for a few people. In fact, it's really just for those who have not been able to break free from the bondage of guilt, shame, secret addictions, self-debasement, fear, generational curses, an unforgiving spirit, anger, eating disorders, unresolved grief, or depression. This message is for those who are bound by invisible chains that have kept you in spiritual, mental, emotional, physical, and/or financial bondage.

If you're that person who comes to worship, attends Bible study, or engages in personal devotion and still feel powerless, I have good news for you today. So, if you will turn with me to the book of Acts, together we will discover how no one has to remain in bondage.

I don't believe Tasha Cobbs would mind my using her lyrics to tell you that there is power in the name of Jesus to break every chain. That's my subject.

Do I have any believers in the house today? The title I attached to the text are words to a gospel hit that many of you sing. But, I wonder if we really get the message behind the music. **There really is power in the name of Jesus!**

Tasha was not the first to convey this truth. In fact, it was declared first in scripture. Long before the song was recorded, the Prophet Isaiah made it known, saying, Unto us a child is born, a son is given: and the government shall be upon his shoulder: and His name would be called Wonderful, Counselor, the mighty God, the everlasting Father, and the Prince of Peace. That's power!

When the angel Gabriel informed Joseph that Mary would have a son, he said, His name shall be called Jesus, because He will save His people from their sins. That's power! The record is demons tremble at the name Jesus. That's power!

If that is not enough, and in order that we really understand the power in the name of Jesus, would you allow me to walk you through a few verses of this 16th chapter of Acts that lead up to our text?

On their way to prayer, Paul and Silas were met by a young slave girl who was possessed with a demonic fortune-telling spirit. She was being prostituted by pimps who received money from every person whose fortune she told.

For several days, the young girl followed Paul and Silas, saying, these men are the servants of the Most High God, which show unto us the way of salvation. Even though her facts were accurate, her sarcasm was annoying. So, "**in the name of Jesus,**" Paul cast the demonic spirit out of her. Seeing how Paul and Silas had messed up their hustle, her masters brought them before Roman magistrates who upheld the law.

Accusations of destroying the public peace and endangering the public safety were brought against Paul and Silas. However, the Roman law stated that *no person shall have any separate or new gods; nor privately worship any strange gods, unless the public agreed to it.* This law was the real reason Paul and Silas were imprisoned and bound in chains.

Fast forwarding now to our scriptural text, the record is, at midnight Paul and Silas prayed and sang. One might wonder why they waited until midnight when they and all the others should have been asleep. I contend, rather than act and react as those who have no hope, believers who know the power of Jesus' name understand they can hold out until **midnight**. In other words, instead of immediately going off the deep end, as Quin Sherrer states in her book *A Woman's Guide to Breaking Bondages,* "we learn to **wait to worry**."[1]

Worry is self-imposed bondage. Many of us place ourselves in bondage by immediately worrying about something. Can I tell you something else about worry? Worry is fear and anxiety over something that has not even occurred yet. Even if the doctor gives you an unfavorable diagnosis, you are not so much worried about the diagnosis as you are thinking you're getting ready to die. You haven't even died yet, and you're already worried about it.

You receive an eviction notice, and boy you just get to worrying. But you're still in the house. You don't know what's going to happen between the time you receive the notice and the date they say you must vacate. The Lord knows how to work things out for you. So, my question is, why are you worried? You need to stop and learn to *wait to worry*. Worry also gives Satan permission to *break your spirit.* You need to say to Satan, *You will not break my spirit with worry! I will not panic, even if it means holding out until the third watch of the night.*

I read somewhere that in that culture the Romans measured the night in four watches. The first watch of the night was from 6 to 9 p.m. The second watch was 9 to midnight. The third watch was from midnight to 3 a.m. And the fourth watch was from 3 a.m. to 6 a.m. So, during the third watch, Paul and Silas decided it was time to get to praying and singing.

Those who can make it until the *third watch* are able to say like Job, *"Though you slay me, yet will I trust you."* They testify, *"Nothing can separate me from the love of God, which is in Christ*

Jesus." They rest believing *"the Lord will make a way, yes He will."* Before the *fourth watch*, you might hear them singing *"I can make it. This trial I'm going through, God's going to show me just what to do. So, I can make it until the third watch of the night."*

To wait until the *midnight* hour says you have positive expectations in spite of negative evidence. Hence, it was midnight, or during the third watch of the night, that prayer and praise went forth.

How many of you know, even though prayer and praise go hand in hand, that praise is not the norm in prison? Naw, you're not going to hear anybody jumping up shouting "hallelujah" in prison, unless they're in a worship service. But, they will pray. Do you know people will pray when they get locked up? The Lord hears from folks who He never heard from before, when they get locked up. But, offer praises, when the cell doors clang shut—I don't think so!

The Bible says if we pray **with thanksgiving** we will receive peace that passes all understanding.[2] The Bible also says, in everything give thanks, for this is the will of God in Christ Jesus concerning you.[3] I did say in everything. I did not say for everything. We are not thankful for a lot of stuff that happens in our lives. Am I making any sense in here? Oh, I can name a lot things for which I am not thankful. But in the midst of those situations, we ought to be able to say, Lord, I thank You that it is not any worse than it is. We ought to be able to say, Lord, I thank You that I realize it could have been the other way. Lord, I thank You that I know you are working this thing out for me.

You might not be behind bars, but if you want peace while in your personal prison, you better **learn to pray and praise**. Pastor Moore, what do you mean, "my personal prison"? I mean what I said. Whether or not we care to admit it, many of us are imprisoned by our own habits. We know some of what we eat, drink, do, and pursue is not good for us. We know that. But, because we become slaves to our habits, we eat, drink, do, and pursue what we want anyway.

Not only are we imprisoned by our habits, but our thoughts can also imprison us. Some of us hold so closely to our idiosyncratic beliefs until you can't pry us open to alternatives, to suggestions, or even to the truth. If it's in our minds, we think it's just the truth anyhow. We need not think we are the last word and authority on any and every subject. Nobody knows everything!

Now, I do personally know people who are not only prisoners of habits or imprisoned by their thoughts, but I know people who are prisoners of fear. They have phobias. They won't even venture out of their own homes because they are afraid somebody is going to get them or do something to them. Now, people do crazy stuff now, but you don't have to live and walk around in fear. It would be a travesty not to trust God enough to just get on up and do what you have to do and go where you have to go.

Maybe you missed the latest memo. But if these knuckleheads want what you've got, they will come into your house with you sitting there with your ankles crossed, while you're eating your Sunday supper. So, you'd better pray and call on the name of Jesus; get yourself up and go on to church, go on to the grocery store, go on to the banquet, go on out of town, go on wherever you need to be, and stop sitting there babysitting your house. It's just stuff anyway!

And then, there are some more folks who are in bondage to one way, pseudo, injurious relationships, just for the sake of companionship. So they maintain fellowship with somebody who they already know is not good for them. They just sit and accept abuse. They sit and live in bondage, bound to the core, because they don't want to give up these folks that mean so much to them. I don't understand it for the life of me, but can I help you today? The Bible warns us about being unequally yoked. In another place, it asks the very profound question, *How can two walk together unless they are in agreement?*

Here, Paul and Silas *are in agreement.* They travelled together. They preached together. They spoke the same language and taught the same thing, because they both loved the Lord, which got them thrown into prison, together. I can't think of anybody better to be imprisoned with or chained to than somebody who is of the same mindset as I am, somebody who loves the Lord like I do. I can't think of a better person. In other words, I need to tell you today you need to watch the company you keep!

Look at your neighbor and say, I'm here, and you're here. I believe we're in good company! Together, Paul and Silas prayed and sang so loudly that the other prisoners heard them. And suddenly a great earthquake shook the foundations of the prison. Immediately all the doors flew open, and all the prisoners' chains fell off. I'm telling you, **there is power in the name of Jesus to break every chain.**

In spite of strongholds that could have broken their spirits, this dynamic duo sent up prayers and praise *in the name of Jesus.* Now, if you've been unsuccessful breaking free of bondage, you need to find yourself a prayer and praise partner to call on the name of Jesus with you. And tell the devil, *You will not break my spirit.*

Not only should you **wait to worry**, and **watch the company you keep**, but it is also important to *win the battle in* *your mind.* You have to believe when you call on the name of Jesus that He will work a miracle on your behalf.

I have a relative who was in bondage to drugs for over 20 years. He was tired. He was in and out of rehab. He didn't like himself and what he was doing. He cried out for the prayers of the saints. When I realized he was really serious, in my prayers for him I would say the same thing every day. I would say, Lord, today just might be the day that he will be free of his bondage. In other words, *in my mind I saw the battle won!* I just didn't know when and I didn't know how. But I knew in my sanctified spirit that the Lord would break every chain. I couldn't put a time frame on God, but I had faith in God. As Christians, we are called to see those things that are not as though they are. You need to *win the battle in your mind.*

The prisoners were not the only ones who heard Paul and Silas. Somebody else heard them too. I believe God heard their prayers and their song. Somebody said God was so pleased with the prayers and the praises of Paul and Silas that God Himself shouted *Amen* and caused a great earthquake!

The earthquake caused the prison guard to be awakened. For a prison guard to be awakened by the earth quaking, the prison shaking, the doors flying open, and chains falling off, that was a nightmare. Thinking all the prisoners had escaped, he was about to commit suicide, because he knew the penalty for allowing prisoners to escape was his own death. Rather than being executed, Roman jailers preferred taking their own lives. But what this guy didn't realize was somebody greater than he was in control of the situation. But Paul, who was aware said, *"Brother, don't harm yourself; we're all here."* The jailer then went and fell down, trembling, at Paul and Silas's feet.

I heard demons will tremble at the name Jesus. **That's power!** This was a tough guy (not a wimp). In other words, the power of the name of Jesus will weaken the power of the enemy. The enemy is anything or anybody that holds you hostage, keeps you in bondage, and hinders your freedom.

I understand the guard was probably a retired *Roman soldier.* Yet, here he is falling down at Paul and Silas's feet asking them, "What must I do to be saved?" They said, "Believe on the Lord Jesus Christ, and you shall be saved." It's true that there is *power in the name of Jesus to break every chain.* But, *there's also an army rising up* to break every chain.

The preachers said to the soldier, a man who had been in the army, "If you believe on the Lord Jesus Christ," not only you, but your entire family will be saved. That's what you do when you're in the military. You don't leave anybody behind. You bring them along with you.

When you call on the name of Jesus His *army will rise up* to tear down barriers that have blocked your freedom of worship, your freedom of praise, your freedom of peace, your freedom of joy. Call on the name of Jesus and He will release an army of strength to take the enemy down. Call on the name of Jesus and He will break every chain!

I don't know about you, but I think I hear something. What's that I hear? What's that I hear? **I hear the chains falling.** I hear chains of depression falling. I hear chains of doubt falling. I hear chains of fear falling. I hear chains of addictive behavior falling.

Chains of guilt are falling. I hear chains of anger falling. Chains of envy and embarrassment are falling. I hear chains of loneliness, resentment, overwhelming grief, and nervousness falling. I hear the *chains* falling. I hear chains of financial bondage, chains of physical and family bondage falling.

One day my chains fell. Today just might be your day. I don't know when your day will come. But, I know there is power, power, *power in the name of Jesus*.

Most of all, when you call on the name of Jesus, you will hear broken chains of sin falling. They will fall, because there is power in the name of Jesus to break every chain. It doesn't matter what has you bound. It doesn't matter what has you shackled. It doesn't matter what has you handcuffed. There is power in the name of Jesus.

Somebody just needs to call His name. Jesus! Jesus! Jesus! If you're tied (t-i-e-d), call His name. If you're tired (t-i-r-e-d), call His name. If you're sick of the shackles that have you bound, I dare you to call Him. Jesus, in the morning! Jesus, in the noonday! Jesus, in the evening! Sweet Jesus, at midnight, the *third watch* of the night; just call His name, Jesus!

The Bible declares there is no other name under heaven given among men whereby they must be saved, except the name of He who came to preach deliverance to the captives, recovering of sight to the blind, to set at liberty them that are bruised.

God is releasing somebody today. **Why don't you come?**

NOTES

1. Quin Sherrer and Ruthanne Garlock, *A Woman's Guide to Breaking Bondages* (Ann Arbor, MI: Servant Publications, 1994), 110.

2. Philippians 4:6-7, paraphrased.

3. 1 Thessalonians 5:18, paraphrased.

What Will We Call This Baby?

Shauna St. Clair

BIO. IN BRIEF

Reverend Shauna St. Clair accepted her call to preach at age 19 while studying Biology at Spelman College, in Atlanta, Georgia. Shauna obtained her Master of Divinity from Vanderbilt University and was awarded the Umphrey Lee Dean's Award. In 2011, Shauna was licensed to Ordained Ministry by the Georgia Region Christian Church (Disciples of Christ) under Reverend Dr. Cynthia L. Hale. Currently, Rev. St. Clair serves as a minister at Ray of Hope Christian Church (DOC) and is completing a Doctorate of Philosophy in Public Health at Emory University focused on implementing large-scale public health policy and environmental changes in faith-based organizations.

Luke 1:19-23, 57-60 (New Revised Standard Version)

The angel replied, "I am Gabriel. I stand in the presence of God, and I have been sent to speak to you and to bring you this good news. But now, because you did not believe my words, which will be fulfilled in their time, you will become mute, unable to speak, until the day these things occur."

Meanwhile, the people were waiting for Zechariah, and wondered at his delay in the sanctuary. When he did come out, he could not speak to them, and they realized that he had seen a vision in the sanctuary. He kept motioning to them and remained unable to speak. When his time of service was ended, he went to his home.

Now the time came for Elizabeth to give birth, and she bore a son. Her neighbors and relatives heard that the Lord had shown his great mercy to her, and they rejoiced with her.

On the eighth day they came to circumcise the child, and they were going to name him Zechariah after his father. But his mother said, "No; he is to be called John."

"Sticks and stones may break my bones but words will never hurt me." This is one of the many chants from my childhood that helped propagate the myth that the names we are called don't really matter. But time and time again, history, current events, and our life experiences tell us otherwise. Our dark U.S. closets reveal that there were names that were consequential; names like Toby. As shown in the movie *Roots*, Toby is said to be the American name ascribed to an enslaved African man as they tore his black body with whips until birth names like "Kunta Kinte" could no longer be found on his lips.

And there are names like "alien." If one is called "American settler," "pioneer," or "immigrant" we recognize the valor in their quest to secure life liberty and the pursuit of happiness for themselves and their children. But there are those called "aliens," illegal aliens at that. Propaganda about so-called unalienable rights is preached to those who are called "citizens," and divisive barbed wire fences are built to meet "illegals" at our borders—all to protect the often-illusive American Dream.

They call them ratchet, video vixen, thug, and gangsta. These names are doused liberally upon young black girls and boys in efforts to convince them that their value is based on how well they twerk, how good they are in bed, how quickly they can make easy money, and how fast they can spend it on things that don't last. The names they call them intend to track them into unstable homes, illegal jobs, overflowing prisons, and dead-end destinies.

We have seen the harsh realities and results of bad names and labels, but then there are those life-changing, redeeming, transformative moments when someone declares our name to be what God has called us to be. It's simple titles like "Ma'am" and "Sir" that have pulled down societal strongholds set up by names like "gal" and "boy." These titles of honor ring out in families, churches, and schools to remind the women and men graced with years and wisdom that we respect their roles in our communities.

There is medicinal-like meaning in a label like "Doctor." Yes, it was one high school counselor who called a boy doctor before he was old enough to earn that label that triggered a melting away of academic labels like "special ed.," "trouble student," "hyper-active," and "loser." One prophetic counselor calling him doctor helped restore a young man's self-worth enough to let him achieve everything necessary to walk across a hardwood stage in a black robe with three chevrons on his sleeves. That day they would have to call him doctor instead of dumb.

I remember when they began to call me Reverend. It was after my ordination service. I was almost brought to tears just thinking about the awesome responsibility and privilege of proclaiming the good news of God's love and redemption. And

I remember thinking how meaningful this new title was to all the women and men who struggled before me to carry out their calling, but were denied being called Reverend because of their gender or race.

Our society and our history give us far too much evidence to buy into the myth that names/words don't matter. Names have meaning. Titles have meaning. We behave based on what certain people call us. We may fight to change what they call us. We may rebel against what they call us. We love or hate what they call us. We strive towards or run away from names and titles, but they matter. What we are called, and what we call others, impacts how people are treated, and profoundly influences who we are, how we live, and what we do.

This important topic of naming is central to the event unfolding in our Lukan passage as Elizabeth and Zechariah gather with friends and family for a long-awaited baby's circumcision and naming ceremony. This is an especially celebratory event because these two parents are in the winter of their life and were not expected to be able to have children. However, Elizabeth and Zechariah are one of a few couples in the Bible that received a divine message from God telling them that despite the evidence of infertility, God would give them a baby.

Since this prophesy was first given to Zechariah and Elizabeth, they and their families have been blessed to watch it come to pass. Between verse 19 where we began reading and verse 57 where we picked back up, we can be almost certain that about 9 months and 8 days have passed. And they have watched a divine promise transition from morning sickness to a bulging belly, to a kicking fetus, to contractions and labor pains, and finally a birth. And God was with them through it all.

The family is gathered because a miracle has happened—a baby boy was born to senior citizens. And, now, on the eighth day of this child's life, his loved ones come to the side of this budding family for the rite of circumcision. It is the tradition that at this time male children also be named. Loved ones present would have recognized the significance of this naming process. It had everything to do with whom they believed this child would be. The poignant question that centers this familial gathering is what will we call this baby?

Fortunately, this family has been prepared to answer this question. Both Zechariah and Elizabeth received a divine cheat sheet concerning the baby's name before Elizabeth had even conceived. Month's prior, Zechariah, a priest, was in the temple of the Lord burning incense when an angel, Gabriel, gave him a divine word about the son to whom Elizabeth would give birth. Zechariah was told that he and Elizabeth would have a child and his name was to be John, which means "God is gracious."

Zechariah is to call his son John, and to raise him with the instructions that the angel gave him along with the name. John will be special, so he doesn't get to drink wine or do what everyone else does. This child has to stand out, so his parents have to rear him differently.

Zechariah is to call his son John and claim the prophecy that was spoken over his life with his name. John is to be filled with the Holy Spirit even before he is born. He will bring back many people of Israel to the Lord their God. And he will go on before the Lord, in the spirit and power of Elijah, to turn the hearts of parents to their children and the disobedient to the wisdom of the righteous to make ready a people prepared for the Lord. John's name means "God is gracious." And he is to live into that name.

What an amazing gift God has entrusted to Elizabeth and Zechariah. The revelation of who his son would be was so awesome to Zechariah that he thought, *God must have the wrong people; there is no way God has something that big in store for me and my wife.* Zechariah doubted God, thinking surely God must have all that rearing stored up for some younger, smarter, and more qualified couple. Because of Zechariah's doubt, God silenced his mouth until the prophecy came to pass. And so silently he watched God show up and allow two old, barren people to have a baby that God said should be called John.

Fortunately, for John (and for us) God has a habit of giving names and gifts that are bigger than we can imagine or deserve. God has a way of reminding us that God is able and willing to do exceedingly and abundantly above all that we can ask or imagine. Even if it doesn't seem humanly possible; even if we cannot comprehend how in the world it could be done, God does it.

Oh, the promises of God are so vast, so amazing, so big, that at times they push us to disbelief and even silence us. Still, God's promises go forth. Drawn from the loins of a silent husband and barren wife, God brings forth a child to carry a message of hope that a Savior is near.

A miracle baby, whom God has called John before he was even conceived, now sits in a circumcision and naming ceremony in the arms of his parents among a host of family. And concerning the miraculous calling embodied in this baby, the question is posed, **What will we call this baby?**

I am not a mother. And I suspect that several of us here do not have children or the experience of naming a child. But, within this text, I think there exists an issue with which each of us can identify. Many of you know what it feels like to want something that everyone says is nearly impossible to have. We can remember the moments when something we yearned for was just a glimpse, a far-fetched idea, a passion, a hope, or maybe even a fear of something amazing … a call.

Some of us can understand Elizabeth and Zechariah in this moment because you have watched something that began as an idea grow through difficult circumstances into something real. What was a joy for helping people learn has manifested into you actually having a classroom of students of your own. What was once a longing to help improve your community has resulted in you running your own non-profit. For so long it was a seemingly impossible dream you worked towards, but now you are the thing for which you hoped. You are the employee or boss. You are the preacher, teacher, lawyer, executive, or professor. You are the husband, wife, or parent. You are the very thing you prayed so hard to become. God has delivered as promised. And you are forced to answer the tough question—what will you do with it now that you have it? What will you call this baby? In other words, how will you treat the gifts you have been given? Your treatment will tell the world and God what you think about the gifts—your actions will tell on you. People can watch you and tell how you feel about your gifts.

Elizabeth and Zechariah were told what to name their baby, although their relatives didn't know it. Now, here stand you and me gazing into the eyes of a miraculous, unwinding, unwieldy gift with the unavoidable question—what in the world will I do with this gift from God? **What will we call this baby?**

Later in the text we see how Elizabeth and Zechariah respond to this very question. They show us whether they believe what God has promised them and if they will be obedient to raise, nurture, and prepare this gift from God to be all that God is calling him to be. Will Elizabeth and Zechariah take the leap of faith to follow God's calling, or will their efforts to please God cease when they have gotten the gift for which they asked?

We are modern-day Elizabeths and Zechariahs because regularly we stand in the presence of our family, our friends, our world, our colleagues, and our children with gifts bigger than ourselves, and we answer by our actions whether we will allow God to do miraculous works through us that push us into our callings, or let our efforts to please God stop, when we get the things for which we begged. What will we call this baby?

Unfortunately, making decisions to be faithful to God's call is not always a simple thing to do. At times, it can feel as complicated and drama-filled as a family reunion. It is not with calmness or ease that we name this child, but in complexity and ambiguity.

There are three factors that complicate the naming ceremony for Elizabeth and Zechariah's baby boy and can complicate what we name our gifts. First, they are surrounded by family and friends who, while good-intentioned, do not understand their son's promise. Nothing about the text depicts them as anything other than well-intentioned relatives. Still, these well-meaning relatives threaten the calling on John's life because they weren't given his parents' vision. So they only know to name the baby based on what they have seen done in the past. Someone is going to get that after church.

Since Zechariah cannot speak, the family takes on the responsibility of naming the child. They prepare to name him after his father. His father is a good man. He is a priest whom the Bible says was upright in the sight of the Lord. The family was going to name the child Zechariah.

The family and neighbors planned to name Zechariah and Elizabeth's son Zechariah. And maybe this is how it should be. If his parents let them name him Zechariah, he may become a good guy—a priest. He can grow up and tend to the temple like his father. The family will be pleased. Elizabeth and Zechariah can stay safely in their family's graces. And above all no one will be offended. Zechariah, Jr.: it kind of has a ring to it. Name him the way we have always done it. This decision sounds okay, doesn't it? It's not perfect but it makes sense, right? It's not quite what God said to do, but it could work, right?

Zechariah, Jr. can be justified. Perhaps we can convince ourselves that it's right. Zechariah, Jr. sounds familiar and non-controversial. It sounds like pulpits that preach the messages people like to hear, but not necessarily what they need. Zechariah, Jr. sounds like staying on the safe side of the street away from boycotts. It sounds like ignoring those hurtful sexist/racist/homophobic things you heard the guys saying at work to stay in the good-old-boys network. Zechariah, Jr. sounds like keeping your mouth shut in your new promotion but promising that when you get the next one or maybe the one after that, then you will be in the right position to speak truth to power.

The thing about names like Zechariah, Jr. is that they are safe and don't require sacrifice. You don't have to rock the boat. You can keep everyone calm. It means knowing what God is saying but never having to apply it in ways that make a difference. Zechariah is a great name … but it sounds like doing the same thing over and over and over again and pretending that something amazing and new will result. You do know that's the definition of insanity.

What Zechariah and Elizabeth cannot shake though is what they know deep in their souls, which is that God did not tell them to name their baby Zechariah! No, God said that boy's calling is bigger than filling his dad's shoes. His name is supposed to be John.

Will anyone speak up? Who will speak against the status quo that seeks to rename this boy? Who will put into action God's promise to send a messenger to prepare the way for our Lord?

Somewhere…somewhere deep within the heart and soul of a mother named Elizabeth stirred the response. NO! HIS NAME IS TO BE JOHN. Somehow, in first-century Palestine, despite the depths of patriarchy that should have drowned out this womanish defiance, something stirred resistance from Elizabeth's lips. What made this woman raise her voice to counter the popular movements of her day? What urged this woman to reject the "good name" given to her son by the people who rejoiced with her when they found out she was an expectant mother? Elizabeth, what made you speak?

I believe that Elizabeth spoke because she understood that this gift, this amazing gift, was not just for her and her husband. She was not given a son to prove that she could give birth. Elizabeth took on the risk of losing friends, upsetting family, and being ostracized for her outspokenness because she was entrusted with a gift from God that was supposed to change the world. Filled with the Spirit—for herself—for her baby—for her family—for her community—for her world, Elizabeth cries out with reckless abandon. No! His name is to be John.

The second thing that makes this naming ceremony difficult is that when Elizabeth does what God says to do she encounters rejection from those who are closest to her. The text says Elizabeth's family and neighbors turn to Elizabeth and say, "But there is no one in your family by that name." In essence, Elizabeth, this whole John thing is silly. That idea can't be right because we have never seen it done before. Please take your out-of-the-box idea somewhere else so we can finish naming **your** baby.

We learn from Elizabeth that sometimes carrying out the calling God places on our lives will require us to sit in a crowd of well-intentioned people who tell us that we are crazy, misguided, or harming a worthwhile tradition. They may even reject our ideas and us. God's promise is different and unfamiliar, but Elizabeth knows that her baby's name is supposed to be John and he is supposed to prepare the world for a savior.

While Elizabeth is still standing there, her family does the inevitable—they go over her head to her husband. Zechariah, your wife is over here coming up with all these strange ideas. You saw us reject her crazy idea, now what do you say this boy's name should be? We say he should be named after you.

Can we pause here for just a moment? Before you allow yourself to assume that you are the overlooked Elizabeth in this passage, let's consider for a moment that you are instead Zechariah. In a world where isms such as racism, sexism, ageism, and heterosexism drive power, status, and decision-making, what will you do in the moments when you have Zechariah's privilege? How will you side when you have something personal to gain by going against the most vulnerable in your group? Within Zechariah's patriarchical society it is his maleness and perhaps his age that gives him a dominant position and allows him to overrule Elizabeth. In your experiences perhaps it will be your prestigious college degree or your street cred'. Perhaps it will be your older age or your desirable youth that gives you your advantage. When you have position and status. When you have something to lose. When your pride is on the line. When there are perks in it for you if you help maintain the status quo. When justice is at stake, will you go over Elizabeth's head, or will you be an ally?

The question lies in Zechariah's court. What will you call this baby? Zechariah cleared his throat to respond but no words came out. Zechariah still can't speak. The angel said that he would be silent until the prophecy came to pass…and because this child still has no name and there has been no public claiming of God's promise for their child's life, his lips remain sealed.

The third reason this naming ceremony is difficult for this baby's parents is precisely because his father can't talk. Man! Here we are trying to name this baby like God told us to but the family is acting up, the mother is overruled, and the father can't talk. This is all too much! Perhaps we should just go ahead and give in and call this baby junior after all? If God really wanted his name to be John he should have made it a little easier to do.

I think this is where so many of us get stuck. We assume that if God gives us a gift that everything about putting it to work should be easy. Zechariah could have said, "Well, if God really wanted me to make sure that my son walked into his promise then God would have given me my voice back." If God really wanted me to be a teacher who helped transform the lives of children, he would have given me better teaching supplies. If God really wanted me to be a preacher then he would have given me a church that was more accepting of my calling. If God really wanted me to start that non-profit then he would lead me to someone who has funding. If God really wanted me to make my marriage a Godly model of love and commitment, in a society where over half of marital unions end in divorce, then he wouldn't keep letting these marital hurdles happen. If God really wanted me to make ethical decisions on my job then he would give me better bosses. If God wanted me to…fill in the blank.

Why would God expect a mute man to speak up? If God really wanted Zechariah to speak up for his wife and son, shouldn't he have opened his mouth first? The truth is that sometimes following God's directions, holding to God's promises, and allowing the gifts that God has placed in us to come forth is not easy. Sometimes our journey is burdensome, hard, and nerve-wracking. But we must follow the promises of God anyway.

As we carry out God's calling on our lives we are bound to reach points when it seems nearly impossible to move forward. In these moments the only thing we can be certain of is that God will never call us to do more than he is willing to do through us. What Zechariah will soon learn and what he teaches us is that there is nothing impossible with God. We serve a God who sends stuttering men like Moses to be mouthpieces before pharaohs and to lead a nation to liberation. God will send an oil-bearing prostitute to teach generations to come about holiness and worship. God will take a man like Isaiah who said every word that came out of his mouth was sin and make him one of the most quoted prophets of the Bible.

No, Zechariah still doesn't have a voice, but he doesn't give up because he and his wife believe the promise that God has given them. They believed that God spoke to them. They believed that God made them parents when everything and everyone said they would never have children. They believed God brought that baby through a risky pregnancy. And they believed that God was big enough and faithful enough to grow him into the man God promised he would be . . . a man of God that the Lord could use to turn the hearts of parents to their children and the disobedient to the wisdom of righteousness and to make ready a people for the coming of the Lord. And above all this, Zechariah believed that his son didn't need anyone else to name his baby because God had already given him a name!

No, Zechariah did not have a voice, but he had a piece of paper and something to write with. Zechariah, **what shall we call this baby?** Zechariah scribbles a message with his pen and holds it up for the crowd to see. And to the astonishment of those gathered, on the paper were the words: "His Name Is John."

Immediately Zechariah's mouth is loosed. His first words are praises to a faithful, most-High God. The family members and neighbors gathered are so awe-struck by the miracle that happens when this boy is named that they go out to spread the good news of the infinite possibilities God has in store for a boy named John.

And God wasn't finished with Elizabeth and Zechariah's boy yet. The Bible says that John grew into a man and became strong in spirit. Based on the reports from the Gospels of Matthew, Mark, Luke, and another John, we learn that Zechariah and Elizabeth only knew the half of what their gift from God would grow to become.

Because they named him John and raised him as John, a father's tongue was loosed to speak prophetic words, and witnesses went out proclaiming the good news of God. Who knew that when they called him John he would be the one who cried out from the wilderness and prepared the way for the King of kings, the Lord of lords, a redeeming God made flesh.

What happens when we name our gifts what God has called our gifts to be? Our gifts mature, grow, and touch the people for whom they were given. We call wrongs into repentance and inform our world of resurrection possibilities. What happens when we are bold enough to call our gifts what God has called our gifts to be? We carry out our authentic, innovative callings and prepare the world to encounter God's redemptive grace! So now, I ask you again, **what will you call your baby?**

I Am My Sister's Keeper!

Cherisna Jean-Marie

BIO. IN BRIEF

Reverend Cherisna Jean-Marie is an ordained minister in the Christian Church (Disciples of Christ). An alumni of Vanderbilt Divinity School and recipient of the Florence Caldwell prize for Outstanding Preaching in 2010, she serves as an Associate Minister at New Covenant Christian Church in Nashville, Tennessee.

Luke 1:39-45, 56 (New International Version)

At that time Mary got ready and hurried to a town in the hill country of Judea, where she entered Zechariah's home and greeted Elizabeth. When Elizabeth heard Mary's greeting, the baby leaped in her womb, and Elizabeth was filled with the Holy Spirit. In a loud voice she exclaimed: "Blessed are you among women, and blessed is the child you will bear! But why am I so favored, that the mother of my Lord should come to me? As soon as the sound of your greeting reached my ears, the baby in my womb leaped for joy. Blessed is she who has believed that the Lord would fulfill his promises to her!"

Mary stayed with Elizabeth for about three months and then returned home.

I love this story in the Gospel of Luke. It's one of my favorite stories in the entire Bible.

It's a story about purpose and destiny.

It's a story about submission and obedience.

It's a story about favor and blessings.

It's a story about interconnected-ness, how I need YOU, and you need ME!

It's a story about friendship, sisterhood, respect, honor, and celebration!

I really love this story. It helps us imagine what it could look like if we really lived out the theme for this weekend's Women's Conference: "I Am My Sister's Keeper." Whenever I hear folks say that women can't get along I often wonder if they ever had a chance to read this pericope in the third Gospel in the Bible about two women who lived together for 3 months because they both discovered that they were pregnant with something so much greater than they were! They were two women who discovered that life had purpose and that dreams can come true. It's a story within a story, y'all. It's a story that helps us imagine what can happen when two women come together and realize that God has enough blessings for each of them!

No, there is no hating in this story. No shade throwing. No fear that God is too limited to bless both you and me. No "she thinks she's better than me" in this story. There is no VH1, MTV, or Bravo mess here. This is a story about women who understand that they can never reach their full potential without having other women around them to push them towards their destiny.[1]

That makes me wonder whatever happened to the role of midwives? Women who helped other women push. According to the NOVA Natural Birth Center in Virginia, traditionally women have been the healers in communities. Women held the wisdom of the healing power of herbs and carried the rich oral history of healing from generation to generation. Older women taught younger women how to care for their families and neighbors—thus training the next generation of community healers. Women tended to the sick and the dying, as well as to the birthing mothers in their communities. They were midwives. They helped other women push.[2]

And please don't get lost on this image of a woman being pregnant because I'm not just talking about the physical state of pregnancy. No, I'm talking about being pregnant with purpose. You have been overshadowed by the Holy Ghost and now you are pregnant with a purpose. I'm talking about when you discover that life has so much more meaning because you realize you're about to do something that will change the world! I wish I had some pregnant people in here this morning—people pregnant with purpose. Brothers, I know it is impossible for you to be physically pregnant, but when the Holy Spirit overshadows you…you too can be pregnant with purpose!

But getting back to women, I'm baffled and saddened by the lies that we tend to believe about women. You know the lies:

- Women are catty.
- Women got too much drama goin' on.
- Women don't get along with each other.
- Women can't come together in a group without some form of madness occurring.

I'm more concerned about the lies that are told about black women:

- Black women are angry.
- Black women have attitudes.
- Black women are either hyper-sexual or mammies.
- Black women have a chip on their shoulders.
- Black women are always giving the side eye and throwing each other under the bus.
- Black women shouldn't trust other black women, especially not with what some women believe is their most precious possession—a man!

I'm perplexed by how we can wrap ourselves in these myths and be comfortable with them and perpetuate them when we say:

- I don't really hang out with sisters because of this or that.
- I don't have women friends because of this or that.
- I don't want to work for a woman because of this or that.
- I don't want a woman as my pastor because of this or that.

Our acceptance of negative caricatures about women give credence to certain reality TV shows, Tyler Perry movies, black urban romance novels, and even silly beauty shop discussions on Saturday mornings.

I don't know about you, but I'm tired of the baseless, buffoonish storylines on the big screen, little screen, and in too many media conversations. Then there is the broken, abused, needy, distorted, damaged woman who doesn't know how to have healthy relationships with anybody. Look at your neighbor and tell them that ain't our story![3]

These are lies, myths, stereotypes, and generalizations that we perpetuate in our own realities. It becomes a self-fulfilling prophecy. We hear it and see it all the time so it becomes part of our make-up when interacting with each other. This leads to the suspicious glance, the phony smile, and the unwelcoming space we create for no reason at all. It's because somebody lied and said whenever women are around trouble is on the horizon. It's because somebody lied and said there is always a threat in the atmosphere whenever women get together.

The problem is that the devil has learned how to manipulate our minds to have us believe that we should be threatened by coming together. But the truth is that the devil and the world are threatened by what happens when we come together and come correct.

Here are some facts we need to know:

- No major movement has happened without women: not the Jesus movement, the Underground Railroad movement, the Women's Movement, the children's rights movement, or the civil rights movement. There is no major movement without the coming together of women young and old who got their hands dirty for the sake of change.

- "Pray the Devil Back to Hell" is a documentary about ordinary women, grandmothers, wives, aunts, sisters, and daughters who got tired of the senseless war in Liberia that took the lives of their people. These women banned together and fought for peace through prayer, sit-ins, and protest in 2003. Great things happen when courageous women come together.

- On January 12, 2010, a 7.0 magnitude quake hit the island of Haiti, killing over 200,000 and destroying communities and homes. It made worldwide news. The stories were devastating. The conditions were horrific! My parents, being from Haiti—you can imagine how it hit home for us. We watched the news and felt guilty and helpless all at the same time. But one early Sunday morning a news reporter shifted his storyline from hopelessness to hopefulness when he reported that after a gruesome night, women rose early in the morning and put on their white dresses and hit the streets singing the songs of Zion. It started with one woman, then another woman, then another, and the streets began to fill with women singing and dancing while grabbing their children to join them. These women came together to shed some hope in a hopeless situation. Who says women can't come together!

I bet you don't have to go too far to find stories about the magic that happens when women are united. I bet right here in this very church there are countless accounts of women gathering where miracles have taken place all because of women whose minds and hearts were in unison!

We are descended from queens—women who understood the benefits of community, who knew how to foster good relationships with others. We come from women of faith, who knew how to call on a power far greater than themselves. These women knew that in order to face the world head-on they were going to need God and "sista" friends to conquer the evil.

Am I my sister's keeper? Somebody say, Yes I am!

This pericope backs up everything I've said. Oh yes, I've been in this text. This text shows that a woman of purpose knows she can't reach her fullest potential without the help of other women. Mary ran to Elizabeth when she realized that she too was pregnant. If you want to achieve your purpose, spend time in the presence of a woman who is doing or has done what you want to do. Sit at the feet of women who can help you build and not tear you down. A woman of purpose is a woman who positions herself in between a woman who is doing what she wants to do and a young girl whom she can inspire while she's on her road to completing her destiny.

If you want to reach your destiny, then you must understand that a destiny realized is a destiny shared with others. Even Jesus didn't bear the cross alone. We are communal beings. None of us is an island. We need each other.

Second, Elizabeth welcomed Mary with celebration. She wasn't threatened by Mary. She wasn't fearful of Mary's baby. She wasn't jealous of Mary. She celebrated this younger sister and her purpose in life. Elizabeth was busy fulfilling her own destiny; she didn't have time to hate on Mary. She understood God's blessings were expansive enough to reach both of them. She celebrated and honored Mary's future. She welcomed her with open arms. Can you just imagine what those 3 months were like? Can you just hear the stories they shared, the traditions passed along? Can't you just see how these two came together to help one another out because they refused to allow jealousy, fear, or hate into their atmosphere?

Imagine what can happen in your life when your environment is free from the evil spirits of fear, jealousy, and hate and you are filled with compassion, honor, and love for other women. How far could we go in our communities, churches, and schools if we all took on the spirit of Elizabeth and welcomed and celebrated other women who are pregnant with purpose? I celebrate you as you celebrate me. I honor you as you honor me. I respect your gifts as you respect mine. Elizabeth welcomed Mary with celebration!

Another thing I want to stress about this passage is that Elizabeth's baby leaped upon Mary's entrance. In other words, Elizabeth responded to Mary's personhood. Who is mentoring you? Who is feeding your spirit? Whom do you allow in your personal space that contributes to your psychological well-being? Your ability to reach your destiny is greatly influenced by the company you keep. The people with whom you surround yourself will speak life or death regarding your purpose. People have the power to speak life into your future or not contribute at all. People can remind you that you have purpose or allow you to forget you are on your way somewhere. Sometimes the journey to purpose can make you weary and whom you are journeying with can determine how far you will go. By whom are you surrounded? Do they make your baby leap? Do they speak to your baby or dismiss your baby? Do they contribute good words, thoughts, and deeds or do they just bring you down? Does your baby leap when you are around them? Surround yourself with people who have the abilities, resources, and will to bring excitement to your journey. You are going to need folks to help make your baby leap when the road gets rough and the going gets tough. Elizabeth's baby leaped for joy when Mary showed up!

Finally, as I reflect on this text, I am also reminded of the need for women to love themselves and the need for all of us to love God. Beloved, you can't love anyone else unless you first love yourself. Truth is you can't love yourself unless you first know and see God within you. Not the god with a little "g" that we created and made an idol for the Church but the true and living God. To love me is to know me, but first you must know and love God! Let's love ourselves. Not in the superficial ways we say we love ourselves by primping and dressing up our outer selves while remaining empty inside. We need the real love that only can come from the God who is love.

So I sincerely ask you, when was the last time you went to the doctor, exercised, and ate healthy? How are you doing emotionally? Have you ever been to a counseling session for the grief, the hurt, the trauma you experienced in life? To love you is to take care of your mind, body, and spirit. We can shout around this church all morning, but I submit real worship occurs when we take the time to care and love ourselves holistically.

Then there is the matter of true worship. True worship is found in how we worship the God within ourselves and the God in other people. Not the "god" we worship to please others. Worship occurs when we please God. I dare you to be courageous enough to find God within yourself first and the grace to look for God in others—in your sisters and in your brothers, in communities where people are different than you. God is present. Brothers, it's time to let go of the idol "god" patriarchy. Sisters, it's time to tear down the stronghold of patriarchy. Get it out of churches, out of our homes, and out of relationships! God is located in both a woman and a man. We are made in the image and likeness of God, both male and female! It's time for us to remove the chains of sexism that rob us of our humanity and ignore the divinity within each of us. True worship happens when we are bold and courageous enough to worship the God within others and ourselves.

So as I close, I ask this very important question. This question is the prerequisite to doing everything I've said today. Do you know God? Do you have a personal relationship with God? I didn't ask if you went to church, I asked if you knew God for yourself!

Perhaps there is a war going on inside of you. A fight from within that won't give you peace. A fight that always seems to get the best of you. Perhaps this war started when you encountered a form of trauma that you've never been healed from: abandonment, abuse, death, grief. This war refuses to let you love yourself or anybody else. It refuses to allow you to trust yourself or anyone else. It refuses to let you submit to mentorship. This war consistently keeps replaying the trauma that you experienced and you just don't have any peace. I'm here to tell you, you can be delivered.

Perhaps you are sitting in this church today and you have some trust issues with women because there was a woman in your life who caused you pain and you never forgave her for that. Now each time you encounter another woman you place that old experience on her, hindering you from building healthy relationships with other women. Deliverance is at the door; will you answer it?

Prayer: To the God who intricately, intimately, and intentionally created us in an image that reflects God's self. To the God who made us communal, relational, and purposeful beings. A God who loves us enough to show us grace and mercy daily, we now pray. We ask you, Lord, to first enter our hearts and minds, help us to confess your Son Jesus as our personal Savior. Help us to see ourselves the way You see us. Help us to be in right relationship with you and ourselves so that we are able to be in right relationships with each other. You are a God who heals, delivers, and sets free. Too many any of us have been chained by life's circumstances. Trauma, disappointments, hurts, and terrors have wounded and weakened us. Darkness has seeped in. Evil has tried to consume us, but you are a God who brings light into dark places, a God who makes demons tremble. You are a God who pulls down strongholds. You are a God of victory, healing, and truth. So we ask you right now Lord to break every chain, heal every broken place, and make the crooked places in our lives straight. Heal, deliver, and set us free. Use each of us to make each of us more like you. We ask this all in the name of Jesus our righteous liberator. Amen!

NOTES

1. Renita J. Weems, *Just a Sister Away: A Womanist Vision of Women's Relationships in the Bible* (Philadelphia, PA: Innisfree Press, 1988).

2. www.midwifecenter/midwives.org.

3. Demetria L. Lucas, "She Matters: Despite what you see on reality TV, the bonds of sisterhood are strong," www.theroots.com.

Only a Penny

Betty M. Lovelace-Ross

BIO. IN BRIEF

Reverend Dr. Betty M. Lovelace-Ross is president of the EnVision Consulting Group, which exists to provide leadership management, education, and outreach services to for-profit and non-profit entities. She currently serves as an Associate Minister at Mt. Olivet Baptist Church, in Columbus, Ohio; as faculty at Trinity Lutheran Seminary in Columbus; and as Associate Provost and Associate Vice President at Capital University in Columbus. She received a doctorate degree in Student Personnel Services, with a concentration in counseling, from VPI and State University in Blacksburg, Virginia.

Mark 12:41-44 (New International Version)

Jesus sat down opposite the place where the offerings were put and watched the crowd putting their money into the temple treasury. Many rich people threw in large amounts. But a poor widow came and put in two very small copper coins, worth only a fraction of a penny. Calling his disciples to him, Jesus said, "I tell you the truth, this poor widow has put more into the treasury than all the others. They all gave out of their wealth; but she, out of her poverty, put in everything—all she had to live on."

Since my daughter was 6 weeks old, I have jogged the streets and tracks of every city, state, and country in which I have found myself. Initially, I began jogging as a form of exercise to assist with losing what some would call baby fat, but 34 years later, I am still jogging. Some may say that it's insane, for I am so driven that I will rise early, usually between 5:30 and 6:00 a.m., put on the appropriate clothing for the morning, and take to the streets. Rain, snow, cold, or fair weather, I am out jogging. Whether it is in the city in which I reside or a city, state, or country in which I am visiting, I jog. And, whether I feel like it or not, it is so deeply ingrained in the fabric of who I am that I cannot help but jog.

As I have jogged the streets, I began picking up the coins I would see along my morning run, and I decided that every coin or bill I found, I would bring to the church. Along my journey of jogging and walking the streets, I would find nickels, dimes, quarters, and on occasion a dollar, but primarily my morning find would consist of pennies.

Many would consider pennies so insignificant that they would not even bother to stop or stoop down to pick them up. In fact, many convenience stores have a small container that sits near the cash register into which you can toss any unwanted pennies, because after all, pennies just tend to get in the way, take up far more space than they are worth, and hold little economic value or purchasing power.

A penny takes 2½ times its value in material and production to make, and many countries, with the exception of the United States, no longer even mint them. That obscure, unwanted coin located around trash receptacles, along the edges of streets, on the floor in the marketplace, in the garage, driveway, almost any building you will enter, more often is left where it is because the general thought is, it's only a penny, so why waste your time to pick it up.

How many of you have them in a jar in a corner, in a dish or container on your dresser, or in the console of your vehicle, just lying there—not necessarily for a purpose but just there because you have yet to determine what you will do with them.

Over the years, I become fascinated by how many are tossed away. I have collected the scratched and scarred coins from their life on the street, bagged them, and turned them over to a trustee in the church with a warning of their condition, to which he replied, the bank would exchange them. Over time, this has amounted to me turning in perhaps $25-$30.

Something as insignificant as a penny—and yet, I am driven to look for them, to retrieve them from their resting places, and to save them because they yet have a designated purpose.

In our series on "Grace Giving," I want to direct your attention to the particular pericope involving Jesus and the woman in the temple. I want us to observe how impressed Jesus is with this nameless woman, whose pedigree we know nothing about. We do not know if she had children, her emotional state, or where she lived. What we do know, however, is that Jesus thought enough of her actions in the temple on this particular day that he would call attention to them; thus calling attention to her.

By the time we reach this text, Jesus has had a number of tense confrontations with the religious leaders. He had dealt with the paying of taxes. He had given the first commandment, "Love the Lord thy God with all your heart, and with all your soul, and with all your mind, and with all your strength" (Mark 12:31). In fact, he even sent us the extra mile and indicated that individuals are to love their neighbor as themselves. Jesus has entertained the question about the Messiah being characterized as the Son of David, and now he finds himself in the temple dealing with the pious religious leaders concerning paying alms.

Jesus is steadily moving toward his final assignment—that of the cross—but until he is marched up Golgotha's hill, there is still work to do. There is still preaching, teaching, and blessings to be given. The alabaster box has yet to be opened and poured over his head, and the woman carrying it, blessed for her deeds. The Lord's Supper has yet to occur.

But, on this particular day, he is in the temple where he finds the scribes, walking around in their flowing robes, searching for the most important seats, and trying to make an impression through their ritualistic religiosity. Their giving was just for show, and it was designed to have others gaze upon them and approve. And Jesus' response to all of this was that "such men will be punished most severely."

There were a number of courts in the Temple—The Court of Israelites, the Court of Gentiles, and The Court of Women. The Court of Women is designated as such not because it is used exclusively by women, but because women were not allowed to proceed farther than this court, except for sacrificial purposes.

It is in the Court of Women that Jesus finds himself. To give you an idea of the size of this space, it is a square courtyard, 233 feet on each side (for comparison, it was close to the size of a football field, which is 360 feet long).[1] Within the Court of Women stood four massive lampstands, each 86 feet tall. All around ran a simple colonnade; against the wall of the Court were the thirteen chests, or 'trumpets' for charitable contributions. These thirteen chests were narrow at the mouth and wide at the bottom, shaped like trumpets; hence their name.

Each trumpet or chest was carefully marked. Nine were for the receipt of what was legally due—the Burnt offering, and sin or transgression offerings, and the building fund. The other four were strictly for voluntary gifts for the poor fund—the outreach fund—which would be like our Rose of Sharon fund.

Jesus is right there! He positions himself near the temple treasury, in the Court of Women, and watches what individuals are tossing in the trumpets. Now, Church, you may as well go on, look at your neighbor, and tell them, Jesus is watching what you toss in the treasure chest!

A nameless woman, who by today's standards would be rejected or snubbed, a woman who in all likelihood was not well-educated, even by Jerusalem's standards, a widow of meager means, enters the court. A woman, who did not have Sunday finery, a woman whose hygiene likely left a lot to be desired—no deodorant, no perfume, no scented soap or body wash. It's safe to assume that she may have even had a body odor. Can I paint the picture? This woman would not have shown up in heels, stockings, a nice dress, and make-up. This is a woman with so little, but she is in the temple. She has made her way to church, not caring about what she looks like. After all, she's in the same place as the King of kings. She's in the house of bread, the house of worship. She has come to the right place and she's here, in the Mt. Olivet Church of Jerusalem.

Jesus is also in the temple, and he can see all of what's going on. Each individual passes by and tosses in their money. He watches the rich casting in of their abundance—their silver, and bronze. As the widow passes by the love-offering trumpet for the poor and tosses in her coins, he watches her as well. This widow catches the attention of the Master; she catches the attention of her Lord and Savior. This nameless woman tosses in two small pieces of copper, the value of which is about a penny, and her giving continues to be talked about and held up as a model more than 2,000 years later!

Now, the question I have for us this morning is why is Jesus so impressed with the giving by this nameless woman? Your initial response may be to restate what scripture has presented. After all, it says that she gave her all, but let's dig deeper to see if there is something embedded beneath the obvious.

The first thing the text suggests about what impresses Jesus regarding the giving by this widow is that SHE GAVE WITHOUT PRETENSE! She did not ask to borrow a silver coin from anyone so that she would look good. She gave what she had, and she gave it genuinely, honestly, and unpretentiously. Can't you see her making her way to the trumpet-shaped chest—with the marking "offering for the poor"? Can't you see others looking at her with their self-righteous noses turned up, whispering under their breath about her appearance? Can't you see them discussing her tattered clothes, the rag she has on her head? Can't you see them whispering that she should be the recipient of the offering and not a contributor? But here she is! The others walk up, heads high, smug looks on their faces, and as they are dropping their money into the receptacles, they announce the amount of their currency.

One by one, they file by—gold in the building fund, bronze dropped in the priest offering, silver coins for the poor people's relief fund. Their money makes a good deal of noise as metal meets metal; each giving, and looking around to see who is smiling or nodding with approval. And then, we have the widow who anxiously makes her way to the chest. She does not have enough coins to place in each of the 13 chests; after all, she only has two small coins, and she places them in the box—for the poor. The lepta (the smallest coins in circulation) she places in the box are worth almost nothing in the eyes of humanity. But these coins, on this particular day, met with the approval of the Master.

Let me put this in context: A leptos is a Greek coin, and its value is 1/128 of a denarius—a denarius was a day's wage—given to a man, because it was truly difficult for a woman to be employed and nearly impossible for a widow. There had been no signing of a Lilly Ledbetter Bill! This is why there was the command that a widow's sons should care for her, and in the event that there were no sons, then it was the responsibility of the Church.

If two lepta are what she dropped in, then one can surmise that there were no sons to help provide for her. She brought the least amount one was even able to give but she brought all of what she had.

Were it not for Jesus, the grace-giving of this woman would have been unnoticed. Her two coins made no noticeable sound. Whatever attention she drew from the spectators was not positive, but Jesus noticed her. And he not only observed her giving, he observed her condition and her heart. She gave without pretense.

I have to admit, Church, that when I began wrestling with this text, I became transfixed by two concepts: giving your last, and giving your all. The text does not say she gave her **last**; it specifically states, she gave her **all**. I then sought two theologians, Elder William Ross and Reverend Caruthers, to obtain their exegetical insights on the concepts of "giving your last" and "giving your all." I'm happy to report that their wisdom was in alignment with mine. To give your **last** suggests that that's all you have at the moment (somebody say...at the moment). To give your last also suggests that you can go somewhere and get more.

The vast majority of us can borrow, or someone out of their mercy will give us a few dollars. Individuals on the street stand and beg with an outstretched cup and someone will come along and drop a few coins in it.

To give my **all,** on the other hand, suggests that I have no idea where the next supply is coming from. It suggests that I have no one to go to, and I have no idea how my needs will be met, but I'm stepping out on faith and I'm trusting and believing that God will take care of my needs. In fact, when you give your all, you do so without thinking or worrying about it. This nameless woman gave all of her resources. She understood that giving was an act of worship. She was giving out of a grateful and thankful heart.

Jesus was right there looking into her heart. As she reached into her bosom and pulled out the tattered handkerchief, the Master was also reaching into her heart and blessing her and letting her know that he had her in the palm of his hand. As she was reaching, so was he, and he took note of her. It's a mighty, good thing, Mt. Olivet, to have the Savior take note of you. Jesus delighted in her giving and said, well done. We make God happy when we are obedient and when we bestow a *grace-giving*. The woman gave without pretense, and her giving impressed the Master.

The second lesson we learn about what impresses Jesus is that THIS WIDOW ENGAGED IN RECKLESS GIVING.

The rich gave out of their wealth, but the woman gave out of her poverty. She put in everything on which she had to live, and while it may have been regarded by some as foolish, Jesus praised it and he praised her. Jesus praised her because she had literally given all her worldly wealth to the God whom she claimed to love. She had no one else to provide for her, and in this act of dedication she became completely dependent on God.

Perhaps as she was giving this nameless widow recalled the promise of God that he would never leave nor forsake her. This widow gave without worrying about where her next supply would come from. This is why Jesus tells us in Matthew 6:25 that we are not to worry or raise questions about "what shall we eat; or what shall we drink; or what shall we wear." The answer he renders as to why we are not to worry is that the pagans chase after all these things but the heavenly Father knows that we have need of them and will supply our needs. His word says, "Seek first the kingdom of God and its righteousness and all these things will be added."[2] Perhaps she had heard these sayings as she had earlier traveled the Jerusalem streets and she now brought them back to memory.

The reality is that God wants to bless you, and wants to bless me, and God's blessing is greater than any dollar amount we can ever drop into a collection plate. It is greater than any check you or I can ever write. The song is still true, "You just can't beat God's giving, no matter how you try."

I have one question, Church, are you going to spend precious time trying to hold on, in the words of Joe Tex, to what you've got, or are you going to live recklessly for God and allow him to be reckless with his blessings? His word is true; he will "open the windows of heaven and pour out a blessing you won't have room to receive."[3] Jesus is impressed with the widow because she gave without pretense, and her giving was reckless.

The third lesson we see in this text with this widow is that HER GIVING WAS SACRIFICIAL. The widow put in only a penny, but it wasn't how much she gave that was important; it was the spirit in which she gave. God is pleased when we give joyfully and sacrificially. God is pleased when our motivation for giving is driven by our love for him. It is not the amount given but the motivation of the giver that is prized in God's economy. Let me hasten to say something else, because there may be some here who will quickly conclude that if the amount is not what God notices, then why all the noise around giving? My response to this question is, *Don't you get it?* If God has blessed you abundantly, then he expects you to give abundantly, and beyond this, he expects even your abundant giving to be sacrificial giving. God is asking, even after you have given what you believe to be a respectable amount, what do you have left? Is this a sacrifice? Is what you have given true giving?

When others gave, their giving made a noise because of the large quantity of coins they were tossing in the trumpet chests, but the contribution this woman made in all likelihood was not heard. But, in God's economy, the *noise* made by her small gift was deafening.

She left unnoticed by all of the others, and in all likelihood, she was not aware that Jesus was watching, but he was, and he called the actions of the widow to the attention of his disciples and said, "The truth is this widow has given **by far the largest offering today**, far more than all the other gifts combined. All the others made offerings they would never miss; she gave extravagantly what she could not afford. She gave her all." Luke 12:34 reminds us that, "Where your treasure is, there your heart will be also." This nameless widow understood that sacrifice was not a matter of giving up, but it was a matter of giving to.

The important thing for all of us to take to heart is not whether man will notice but whether the Master will notice and approve. Does the Master approve of your giving? Ask somebody, does he approve?

We serve a God who knows something about giving your all. We serve a God who knows something about unpretentious giving. We serve a God who knows something about reckless giving. We serve a God who knows something about sacrificial giving. More than 2,000 years ago, there was a Savior, who saw a people unfit to live and not good enough to die. There was a Savior who loved a people who were steeped in sin. He believed these people were worthy of a trip through the corridors of time. He made his way down through 42 generations and found his place in the womb of a young woman. He was born and lived in poverty (parenthetically, this is a word for those who question if he is in touch with our needs). He was among the disenfranchised, he was among the 47% and the working poor.

This Lamb—your God and my Savior—counted it not robbery to give his *all* for the likes of you and me. He gave his *all* so that we might have life and have it more abundantly. Satan thought that he had him in his grips when he looked at the Savior elevated high on a cross on Golgotha's hill. Satan thought it was over. And much like the widow's mite (the penny), he did not look like much hanging there—beaten, bloodied, and bruised—with nails in his hands and feet.

Satan was celebrating. There were even spectators standing around saying that if he had opened blinded eyes, healed the sick, fed the hungry, and raised the dead, if he had done all that, then why couldn't he save himself. There were those who concluded that he was no savior at all but *only* a man. But, what appeared to be his **last** breath, and what appeared to be the **final** drawing of the curtain, was in reality the prelude to a brand new day!

He hung on the cross all day and all night Friday and all day and all night Saturday but, early...early...early Sunday morning, he got up declaring that he had **ALL** power in his hand. Mt. Olivet, ain't a that Good news? That's sacrificial giving! We learn it from this woman and we're saved because of it by our Savior! Glory to God! Only a penny.

NOTES

1. www.Bible-history.com/court-of-women.
2. Matthew 6:33 and Luke 12:31.
3. Malachi 3:10.

DISCIPLESHIP
AND FAITH

From the Cave to the Kingdom

Kecia Decosta Ford

BIO. IN BRIEF

Reverend Dr. Kecia Decosta Ford is currently the senior pastor of the Sharp Street United Methodist Church in Sandy Spring, Maryland, and an Executive Board Member of the Black Clergy Women of the Baltimore/Washington Conference of the United Methodist Church. She is also an Adjunct Professor at The Community College of the District of Columbia. Dr. Ford is a certified Life Coach and the President and CEO of Soul Spa Ministries, which focuses on educating, training, and enhancing the lives and ministerial skills of women in ministry. Additionally, she is the author of *Fishing in Mixed Waters*, a resource on how to evangelize successfully in an increasingly changing world.

Colossians 3:1-4 (King James Version)

If ye then be risen with Christ, seek those things which are above, where Christ sitteth on the right hand of God. Set your affection on things above, not on things on the earth. For ye are dead, and your life is hid with Christ in God. When Christ, who is our life, shall appear, then shall ye also appear with him in glory.

One of the great philosophers, Plato, in his work *The Republic,* used an allegory he titled "The Cave" to compare the effect of education and the lack of it in our nature. In the book, Plato has someone describe a gathering of people who have lived chained to the wall of a cave all of their lives, facing a blank wall. The people watch shadows projected on the wall by things passing in front of a fire behind them, and they begin to ascribe names to these shadows. All they had become accustomed to was in the cave and they did not have the desire to see what was beyond where they were. All they could see were the shadows thrown on the walls of the cave.

Plato suggests that if they had dared to ascend out of the cave, they would see the world for what it is and see how limited their thinking had been. If they ascended up out of the cave, they would never again descend back into the cave.

Many of us are like those prisoners living in the caves of our own mind. We are living in caves, some traps and states of bondage we have created for ourselves, and some states of bondage we have allowed other people to create for us.

This is why the Apostle Paul was always dealing with people's thought life. We can't go forward or backward without thinking it first. The Bible says, "As a person thinks in his or her heart, so is he or she."[1] The truth of the matter is that if our thinking does not line up with what God says, we are destined for a cave. If we continue to carry defeatist attitudes, if we do not allow God to take control of our thought life, we will always end up like the prisoners in Plato's allegory, facing a wall, accepting the reality that the cave determines for us.[2]

So often we are in caves and accept the conditions thereof. We've been in the trauma so long that we put names on the trauma in order to handle it mentally. We make up excuses for our low estate because we are so far down in the trenches that we just cannot fathom another way, another life, another lover, job, or relationship. No, I am not saying that there are not traumas that can knock us down and dare us to get up. It can be hard to get up from rape. It can be hard to get up from being abused as a child. It can be hard to get over losing a child to gun violence. It can be hard to get up after losing a long-term job when you're in your 50s. It can be hard to get up after stage four cancer or AIDS.

But you can get back up. This sermon is designed to tell you how. In our text, Paul is concerned that the church in Colossae is distracted and does not find its sufficiency in Christ. Being distracted by anything that takes your focus off the very power that will take you higher than anything or anyone on earth is a life-threatening problem with eternal consequences. In chapter 2 Paul shares with the church that he wished they understood the amount of care and concern that he had for them and how strongly he wanted them to stay on the right course because he knew that the believers in this church loved Christ.

However, many of them had a tendency to be swayed by any new doctrine or movement that came into their community. So it is with us today. Many of us are trying to do great things in life. Many of us are working hard to make our lives better. We bend over backwards in an effort to save our relationships, rear our children right, and save for a rainy day. We're working hard. Then, media, fueled by greed, tries to get us to believe that we don't measure up unless we look a certain way, drive a certain car, and live in a certain type of house. Even the reality shows (Christian and secular) cause us to wonder if we have the favor of God when we see all of the material things and money that those on the TV have that we don't have. All of this is designed to take our focus off God and our commitment to the ways of God.

This is why Paul is trying to encourage these church members who are constantly encountering and being influenced by people of many walks of life. In Colossae, there are people of different backgrounds, ethnic groups, and faith groups. After all, Colossae was a trading port that drew people from all over. There was Hellenism, which was at the heart of much of the culture; its focus was more on philosophy than Jesus.[3] There were the Judaizers who insisted that one must follow the letter of the Judaic Law. The Gnostics were also on location. They taught that matter is evil and since Christ was in the flesh, he couldn't possibly be God.

Paul did not want the saints to be distracted. To be distracted means one is being pulled in different directions than that on which they should be focused. When the people of God are distracted by fads, fashion, foolishness, the Joneses, the clique, the culture, the drama, the scene, and each new thing, we never conclude that the ways of God are sufficient. We also easily conclude that we are insufficient. We need something more, something faster, newer, shinier, bigger, and better. But Paul writes to let this church and us know, don't fall for the distractions. **We are complete in Christ and Christ is sufficient and all we need.**

The Apostle Paul informs the people that they are in a cave of sorts. A cave is created. It is a chamber developed from some sort of collapse. The cave that many of us are in signifies that there has been a collapse in our spirit. We have submitted to something or someone other than Christ. When we are in caves, we are also submitting to the parameters of the cave.

While I am not taking lightly that there are important traditions and ceremonies to which we ascribe in worship, we create another cave when we become so attached to traditions that they obscure God. To be that attached implies that one is not as free as they can be. The enemy would have us believe that we have to do certain things to get to God. He would have us think that we have to follow certain traditions and routines, follow certain people, behave, and look like certain people in order to get to God. Paul expresses that we have all that we need because, "If you then be risen with Christ Jesus…" (meaning, since we are saved) we are complete. The word "if" here does not imply that one may or may not be in Christ. It speaks to the certainty of our being in Christ if we have accepted him in our hearts.

Now, let me tell you how Paul says we can move from a cave to the Kingdom. First, we must **let our purpose be in God**. In other words, we have to let everything that we do be controlled by God. Perhaps the biggest mistake we make in life is living a life where God is not at the center. God knows that we have to go through life. He already knows that we have to endure the things that we are going through down here. He understands our needs. God knows that we need shelter, food, and clothing. However, we have to keep the main thing the main thing in our lives and that is the purposes of God. The scripture tells us that we have to, "seek first the Kingdom of God and His righteousness, and all other things shall be added unto you."[4]

Your heart, your motivations, your aims must be grounded, focused, and centered on God. Paul is telling the church that everything they do should be done to the glory of God. Everything that you do, let it be for the purpose that God has for you in your life. There are few things more powerful than a man or woman who has found their God-given purpose and is living it out with all of the vigor, power, and joy that they have. They are seeking those things that are above; they are not caught up by the hustle and bustle.

Paul tells us to look to those things where Christ is seated, which is at the right hand of God. Here, the right hand symbolizes strength, power, action, and position. Nothing can keep us from what God has for us and what He wants us to do. This is because of God's powerful right hand.

We must let our purpose be in God, for only what we do for God will last. Too often, we go through life in a mediocre way. Or, we do well financially, but when we have to face ourselves in the mirror, we have to admit that we are empty, confused, and wondering why we are here. Then there are those who are neither mediocre, nor flush with cash; they are just miserable. All of these are states of life for those whose purposes do not come from God and are not connected to God; their purpose is not in God.

We were not put on earth just for jobs, just for positions, just to mark time. God has need of us. God is looking for those who will "co-labor" with him to make the Kingdom come on earth as it is in heaven. You have a role; God has an assignment with your name on it. Are you available?

If you want to live in an excellent way, let your purpose be in God. If you want to find out why you are here and to be filled, let your purpose be in God. And if you want your misery to end, let your purpose be in God!

Then, to move from the cave to the Kingdom, we have to **let our passion line up with our purpose** (verse 2). We have to love the things of God. Paul told the church that they ought to set their affections on God. The Greek word *set* is an action word. Action is required, work, and will. When we set our affections, it means we have purposed in our heart that our focus will be on God and God alone. To *set* is to allow the things of God to move us, captivate us, and give us everlasting joy. Every now and then, we can get a little thrill on earth, but it is ephemeral. It is temporary and passes away. We end up saying like B.B. King, "The thrill is gone." Why not grab hold of the thrill that last forever!

That on which we focus becomes that which moves our hearts and unleashes our emotions. Setting our affections on God implies that we are mentally disposed toward God, and our sentiment is that we are nothing without God. We love God with all that is within us. Our love for God far outweighs our love for others because we have found that there is none like Him. We understand that all the favor we have is because God is alive and dwells in our lives. If God did not exalt us, we would still be in one cave or another. We would not have been where we've been if God was not with us and caused us to make it through safely. God is the one! Let your passions line up with God's purposes for you by setting your affections on Him!

This should be our sentiment, our greatest desire, and our sincere prayer. We should know where our help comes from. We do not have to wonder how we made it over. We know every step of the way it was God! The church at Colossae loved Christ, they loved God, and they loved the fact that He changed their lives. But they, just like us, when the honeymoon period of our salvation passes, can find that our passion for Christ waivers. We want to rendezvous with other things to see if they will excite us and hold our attention.

If our affections are on worldly things, then that is what will control us. Addictions are developed. Habits are created and perversions can persist when we mishandle our affections. Our **passion has to be lined up with our purpose and our purpose has to be centered in God**!

Then, we must let **Christ protect us** (verse 3). We do not expect earthly things to protect us. Yes, we do things to maintain healthiness. Every now and then we may need a little security and we put alarms on our doors. On earth that's smart. We want some protection, but ultimately nothing happens in our lives unless God orders it or allows it. The enemy has to get God's permission to do anything in our lives. If we are not relying on the protection of Christ, we will be sorely disappointed every time.

Every now and then God will allow some bitter rain to come into our lives. We do not want to hear or receive that, but it is true. See Matthew 5:44. God will allow a little turmoil to come our way to strengthen us. Sometimes He will allow us to go through something so that we can find out where we are on our faith journey. God will allow an enemy to raise His ugly head, but that is the time to go for what we know and that is, "Greater is He that is within us than he that is in the world."[5] We have died to the world system though our union with Christ in his life, death, and resurrection. Our lives are held in him. He is our greatest protection.

We cannot be so attached to earthly things that we foolishly believe they will protect us. Many of us end up stuck in caves because we relied on things, people, money, and even our own strength to protect us. However, in the midst of storms, Christ is a certain bridge that can take us over. Christ can protect you from your haters, your addictions, your fears, your failures, and every trick of the devil that comes against you. So, **let Christ protect you**!

Finally, we have to let **Christ produce holiness in us** (verse 4). Paul reminds us that we will appear with Christ in glory. To this church community, glory meant dignity, honor, and weight of character, Christlikeness. These are developed in us as we allow the Holy Spirit to sanctify us. Paul let the Colossians know a few verses back not to let people control them through dictating to them what they could do and eat and where they could go. Many today are trapped by other people's ideas of what God is pleased with and what God considers holy. You must have your own relationship with God. You must cultivate your own love life with the King. You have to lift up God in your own private time in order to develop the faith walk God wants for you.

Since we have risen in Christ from the cave of our former lives, and from relationships that are unedifying, jobs that are unprofitable, and people who do not have our best interest in mind, we have tasted life with Christ and no longer want to acquiesce to the standards of the world. We want holy living.

A rather pompous-looking deacon was endeavoring to impress upon a class of boys the importance of living a holy Christian life. "Why would someone call me a holy man?" the man asked. After a moment's pause, one youngster said, "Maybe it's because they don't know you." We laugh, because we tell ourselves that we know how a Christian acts and we know what it means to be holy.

But I am afraid that when I say *live holy*, too many of you think long robes, long dresses, (long something), no sex, no jokes, no make-up, fasting, hours of prayer, and getting up real early every day to read the Bible. That's not holiness. Those may be some of the things holy people do, but that's not holiness. Holiness comes from the Holy Spirit to hearts that make room for God. Author Jerry Bridges said, "We are 100 percent responsible for the pursuit of holiness, but at the same time we are 100 percent dependent upon the Holy Spirit to enable us in that pursuit. The pursuit of holiness is not a pull-yourself-up-by-your-own-bootstraps approach to the Christian life."[6]

Mother Teresa said, "Holiness does not consist in doing extraordinary things. It consists in accepting, with a smile, what Jesus sends us. It consists in accepting and following the will of God."[7] I don't know about you, but I want what Jesus sends me, I want to do His will, and I want to live holy.

I've been set free from the cave. I've been set free from enemies, things, and from myself. I no longer waddle in the things I've done in the past and I've been set free from my inhibitions, the problems, the turmoil, and the limitations that people put on my life. "He [and she] whom the son sets free is free indeed."[8]

Jesus moved me from the cave to the Kingdom. Has He moved you? If Christ is in your life, you can give Him praise! If He has been there for you when no one else has, shout halleluiah! He moved me from the cave to the Kingdom. It was Christ the hope of glory. Christ is the one who turned you around. He looked beyond your faults and saw your needs. It was Christ lifting you up; protecting you; providing for you. He is the one you can depend on because He does not change. You can move from the cave to the Kingdom because you are what Christ says you are. Your life has been changed in God. He is your heart fixer, soul re-possessor, and life re-arranger.

He's given you a new walk, a new life, new honor, and dignity; shout glory! You are out of the cave because **your purpose is in God, your passion lines up with God's purposes, Christ protects you, and Christ produces holiness in you.** You are a Kingdom walker instead of cave dweller. Amen! Amen! Amen!

NOTES

1. Proverbs 23:7.

2. http://www.princeton.edu/~achaney/tmve/wiki100k/docs/Allegory_of_the_cave.html.

3. For an extensive analysis of the Hellenistic world and the Gnostics, see F. F. Bruce, *Paul: Apostle of the Heart Set Free* (Grand Rapids, MI: Wm B. Eerdmans Publishing, 2000).

4. Mathew 6:33.

5. 1 John 4:4.

6. Jerry Bridges, *The Pursuit of Holiness* (Carol Stream, IL: NavPress, 2006).

7. Quote by Mother Teresa online at http://www.goodreads.com/quotes/203154-holiness-does-not-consist-in-doing-extraordinary-things-it-consists.

8. John 8:36.

A Focused Faith

Lisa M. Weah

BIO. IN BRIEF

Reverend Dr. Lisa M. Weah serves as the senior pastor of
the New Bethlehem Baptist Church in Baltimore, Maryland.
She holds a Bachelor of Science in Civil Engineering from
The University of Maryland at College Park and a M.Div. and
D.Min. from Howard University. She is the CEO of LMW
Enterprises, a member of Alpha Kappa Alpha Sorority, Inc., and
author of *Creative Worship in a Contemporary Milieu*.

Ephesians 2:1-9 (New Revised Standard Version)

*You were dead through the trespasses and sins in which you once lived,
following the course of this world, following the ruler of the power of
the air, the spirit that is now at work among those who are disobedient.
All of us once lived among them in the passions of our flesh, following
the desires of flesh and senses, and we were by nature children of
wrath, like everyone else. But God, who is rich in mercy, out of the
great love with which he loved us even when we were dead through
our trespasses, made us alive together with Christ—by grace you have
been saved—and raised us up with him and seated us with him in the
heavenly places in Christ Jesus, so that in the ages to come he might*

show the immeasurable riches of his grace in kindness toward us in Christ Jesus. For by grace you have been saved through faith, and this is not your own doing; it is the gift of God—not the result of works, so that no one may boast.

I n this text, the Apostle Paul writes to the church in Ephesus not to address any *present* problems within the church, but to give clarity regarding the role of the church in continuing the ministry of Jesus Christ within the world. Rather than reactive insights, he offers proactive insights that are purposed to keep this young church on the right path moving towards its divine purpose.

The Ephesian society in which this church was born offered a plethora of possible erroneous paths. Ephesus was a busy commercial center located at the intersection of several major trade routes. On a daily basis, its growing Christian population was exposed to myriad ungodly social, cultural, and religious influences that threatened the integrity of its mission. In fact, a deeply entrenched demonic stronghold existed within its own borders, as Ephesus was home to the temple of the pagan goddess Diana.

The worship of Diana was so widespread within Ephesus that the Ephesian economy thrived off the commercialization of her image. As recorded in the nineteenth chapter of Acts, the entire city went into an uproar over Paul's visit because of the damage his Christian preaching caused to its pagan economic system.

And so, understanding the climate into which this young Christian church had been birthed, Paul wrote to Christians who were facing tremendous cultural, social, and economic pressure to conform to the ways of an ungodly world.

What does this look like for us today? For some, it's trying to be committed to their Christian convictions, but being cast-out and chastised by friends for daring to be different. Some are trying to kick bad habits and live holy while everyone else in their household is okay with straddling the fence. Still others are trying to honor God with their finances while everyone around them is hoping to hit the lottery and live large.

This is why Paul, in chapter one, said, "For this reason, ever since I heard about your faith in the Lord Jesus . . . I have not stopped . . . remembering you in my prayers." And his prayer was this: "that the God of our Lord Jesus Christ, the glorious Father, may give you the Spirit of wisdom and revelation, so that you may know him better" and "that the eyes of your heart may be *enlightened*."

But what did he want them and what should we be enlightened about? We are to be enlightened to the fact that we live in a society that has no place for God—so *we* have been called to keep God in His rightful place in our lives. We are also to be enlightened about the fact that we live in a city that exalts culture above Christ—so *we* have been called to honor Christ above culture. We are to be enlightened to the fact that we live in a society that has set aside the standards of God—so *we* have been called to reset the bar. Once we claim we are Christians, we can't live like everybody else. We can't carry ourselves like everybody else, we can't talk like everybody else, and we definitely can't walk like everybody else. Why? We can't mimic the world because we cannot follow *Christ* and walk in the ways of the *world* at the same time. We cannot minister with integrity and yield to a culture of compromise at the same time. And we cannot maintain a biblical ministry and conform to the seduction of a secular age at the same time.

Paul reminds the believers in verse three of our text that yes, *"All of us"*…lived among them at *one time*, gratifying the cravings of our sinful nature. We've all "been there and done that." Nonetheless, at some point in our lives, a man named Jesus came along. He picked us up and turned our lives around so that while we may not *yet* be who we ought to be, by the grace of God we are not who we *used* to be.

And so, Paul says, we need to be certain we understand that God's grace has not only saved us from the *penalty* of our sins, but also from the *power* sin had over our lives. If we don't understand and appreciate the fullness of what God's grace has done in our lives, we will take it for granted, lose our focus, and allow our environment to entice us back into our old, ungodly ways. How can we be sure this will happen? We can look at these examples:

- Adam lost his focus and sin entered the world.
- Lot's wife lost her focus and turned into a pillar of salt.
- Esau lost his focus and forfeited his inheritance.
- Aaron lost his focus and created a golden calf.
- Miriam lost her focus and was struck with leprosy.
- The sons of Aaron lost their focus and were consumed by strange fire.
- Samson lost his focus and lost his hair and his strength.
- Saul lost his focus and was stripped of his throne.
- Peter lost his focus and started to sink in a sea.
- Judas lost his focus and sold out our Savior!

If we look at our world today, the evidence suggests that the *Church* has lost its focus, as it has become harder and harder to distinguish those who claim to know Christ from those who do not. The evidence also suggests that the Church has lost its focus, as it has become harder and harder to distinguish congregations from social clubs. Likewise, the evidence suggests that *we* have lost our focus, as there are too many preachers focused on prosperity and pandering instead of preaching to increase the social position of our people.

Our text compels us to pause to consider the following questions: Has our faith lost its focus? In other words, has singing our own song become more important than singing the Lord's song? Is carrying out our own intentions more important than carrying our cross and following Christ?

Paul makes clear that if the Church is going to be the Church of Jesus *Christ*, it has to stop emulating an ungodly culture like a Church gone wild, and instead cultivate a *focused* faith whereby its *witness* will be authentic, its *walk* will be empowered, and its *works* will be effective.

Paul reminds the saints that, "God, who is rich in mercy, made us alive with Christ even when we were dead in transgressions." This means that to cultivate a focused faith, we must first **remember what the Lord has already done.** Spiritual ingratitude is a by-product of spiritual amnesia. The only reason anyone could possibly sit in God's house and not give God praise is if they have forgotten what God has already done in their lives.

Some folks only give God praise because they believe that when praises go up, blessings come down. However, if we're going to maintain a biblical ministry in a secular age, we need to stop using praise as a tool of manipulation to try to move God to bless us. Instead, we need to recognize that God is still worthy of our praise because of what He has already done. Even if God never does anything else for us, by saving us, He's done enough!

It's a dangerous thing to forget what the Lord has already done, what he brought us out of, because we are bound to repeat what we fail to remember. That's how we end up falling back into the same stuff over and over again—going back into the same disastrous relationships, or going back into debt, or failing to be responsible over and over again—we forget how much it took for the Lord to bring us out the last time.

Paul implores us not to forget that it is by *grace* that we have been saved, through *faith*—and this is not of ourselves. It is a gift of God, not given in response to our works so that no one can boast. He says this because another by-product of spiritual amnesia is spiritual arrogance. Spiritual arrogance goes beyond ingratitude because *ingratitude* says, "I failed to properly thank you for what you did for me," but *arrogance* says, "I really didn't need you to do anything for me in the first place."

Spiritual arrogance implies that our behavior was perfectly acceptable—even though the Bible says that *all* have sinned and fallen short of the glory of God. Spiritual arrogance implies that we could have picked ourselves up and turned our own lives around, although the Bible is clear that "even when we would do good, evil is always present."

In addition to remembering what God has already done, Paul says that to cultivate a focused faith we must **respect who God is**. He reminds the church that God is the God of great love, and He is rich in mercy. Paul recognizes that the Ephesian church exists within a secular society, where creating lifeless images of pagan gods is the *norm*. Thus, he reminds the church of the divine attributes of the true and living God in order to keep it from conforming to the societal norm and making God into a mere metal ornament. Paul seeks to keep the Ephesian church from becoming desensitized to who God is.

The story is told of a woman who walked into a jewelry store to purchase a necklace and told the salesman behind the counter,"I'd like a gold cross."After looking over the stock in the display, the salesman asked,"Do you want a *plain* cross, or one with a *little man* on it?"Clearly, this man had no understanding of the importance of the symbolism of either piece, but the story underscores exactly what Paul is saying to the Ephesians. If we are to maintain a biblical ministry in a secular age, we have to resist the temptation to turn a *great* God into a *little* man.

Without a focused faith, we will forget that Jesus was fully man **and** fully God; the Alpha **and** the Omega; the Beginning **and** the End; the Lily of the Valley **and** the Bright and Morning Star. Without a focused faith, we will forget that **our** God is the God who stepped out of nowhere, onto nothing, and created everything that is. Without a focused faith, we will forget that **our** God is the God who woke us up this morning and started us on our way; put breath in our bodies and granted us the activity of our limbs; put food on our tables and clothed us in our right minds!

Paul says, without a focused faith you will not only forget what God has done, but you will fail to respect Him for Who He is. He is more than just a religious leader. He is Adonai—the Lord our God; Yahweh—the Lord God Jehovah; Elohim—God our Creator; El Shaddai—the all-sufficient God; He is El Elam—the everlasting God; El Gibbor—the Mighty God; El Elyon—the most high God. There used to be a day when we treated God as such. Perhaps the reason the world doesn't respect the Church as it used to is because the Church doesn't respect God the way it used to.

Finally, in addition to reverencing Who God is and remembering what He has already done, Paul says that we can cultivate a focused faith by **refusing to live beneath God's standards.** Verse 6 says, "And God raised us up with Christ and seated us with Him in the heavenly realms in Christ Jesus." Paul is saying that before we can get clarity on our *purpose* in the kingdom we need to understand our *position* in the kingdom. If we don't understand our position, we will never realize our potential.

The small African antelope known as the Impala is only about three feet tall fully grown, yet it has the ability to jump to heights over 10 feet and cover distances greater than 30 feet within that jump. Despite its tremendous potential, however, the Impala can be kept in any zoo enclosure that has at least a three-foot wall. Why? Because the Impala will not jump if it cannot see over an enclosure to tell where it will land when it jumps.

Like the Impala, many of us have been living beneath the place God has for us because we've been enclosed in our environment instead of focused in our faith. We are afraid to "jump" to move up and out, because we are unsure where we will land. But with a focused faith, we can move ahead, because we know that we really can do all things through Christ who strengthens us. We really can move mountains, or mount up on wings like an eagle. We can walk and not grow weary; we can run and not faint.

With a focused faith, we can maintain a biblical ministry, even in a secular age.

We can stand firm when everyone around us is conforming to the culture, and shoot for the high standard when others around us keep lowering the bar. With a focused faith, we can press towards the mark as our society ignores the mark.

We can choose to remain focused in spite of pressure to be politically correct, culturally correct, or socially correct. Like Joseph, we can make it from a pit to the palace. Like Moses, we can make it through 40 years in an unfriendly land. We will possess our Promised Land like Joshua, and defeat giants, as did David. Like Solomon, we can build something amazing. Like Nehemiah, we can restore broken walls, or receive tremendous joy for our sorrows, like Job. Like the three Hebrew boys we, too, can come through the fire unsinged—with a focused faith!

Just like Jesus, the pioneer and perfecter of our faith, who for the joy set before him, endured the cross, and sat down at the right hand of the throne of God. Just like Jesus, who, being in very nature God, did not consider equality with God something to be used to his own advantage; rather, he made himself nothing by taking on the very nature of a servant, and allowing himself to come to us in human form. And being found in appearance as a man, he humbled himself by becoming obedient to death—even death on a cross! Therefore, God exalted him to the highest place and gave him the name that is above every name, that at the name of Jesus every knee should bow, in heaven and on earth and under the earth, and every tongue acknowledge that Jesus Christ is Lord, to the glory of God the Father! (Philippians 2:5-11)

Amen, and thank God.

Who's Got Your Ear?

Bernadette Glover

BIO. IN BRIEF

Reverend Dr. Bernadette Glover, a native of Scotch Plains, New Jersey, loves ministry and is an interpreter of church and social issues. A graduate of Eastern University, Palmer Theological Seminary (formerly Eastern Baptist Theological Seminary), she holds a doctorate of ministry degree from United Theological Seminary, where she studied as a Jeremiah Wright, Molefi Asante, Cornel West Fellow. Dr. Glover is interim Pastor at St. Paul Baptist Church in Montclair, New Jersey, and teaches Preaching at New Brunswick Theological Seminary as Associate Professor of Preaching and Worship. In 2010, she released her latest book, *Whispers Overheard*, published by Xulon Press.

Luke 4:1-2 (New Revised Standard Version)

Jesus, full of the Holy Spirit, returned from the Jordan and was led by the Spirit in the wilderness, where for forty days he was tempted by the devil. He ate nothing at all during those days, and when they were over, he was famished.

I always have to get myself in a certain frame of mind to go to the eye doctor. A part of the time there bothers me. What I can't stand is when the ophthalmologist shines that light in my eye and gets all up in my face. I want to say, "Back up a bit, I don't know you that well." The more I wish the ophthalmologist would back up, the longer she looks in my eye. So, I asked the doctor what was the light all about. The doctor said to me, "With this light, we see the back of the eye. We get to see the inside of the eye and look for different things. We can see the health of the eye." So, I guess that light is necessary.

This word **if** disturbs me almost as much as that light. I don't know if you have ever had somebody get in your face with an **if**. The word **if** can feel like involuntary scrutiny has come and that it's piercing right through you. Something in you feels like you want the other person to back up. It can feel intrusive, like an examination of your credentials or something. It can be disturbing. **If** is a word that when used in certain circumstances, although you may present a calm demeanor, the hairs on back of your neck begin to ball up like a tight row of miniature fists. The trouble with the word **if** is that when someone uses it a certain way, it presumes that the one asking has the authority to authenticate whether you are or are not, did or did not, can or cannot. It suggests that there is some claim out there about you that only this person can verify. So, it can upset you.

It can cause your defenses to rise up before you know it in a knee-jerk reaction. There are many altercations that have erupted all because somebody crossed the line and either said "if" with their mouth, or with their eyes by cutting them, or they implied it with a gesture. So, depending upon the circumstances, when we hear the word **if**, it can register the idea, "you are not until I say so."

I think maybe the issue is not simply the fact that the speaker is acting out of some inflated sense of authority, but the issue is really who told you so to begin with. "**If you are the Son of God**, then given your circumstances, why don't you be who you say you are and change the situation?" The issue here isn't so much the devil wanting to validate Jesus, as much as it is the devil attempting to throw into question who said He was the Son to begin with. It's not the title; it's the authority behind the title.

Let me explain it this way. You have a driver's license but your license isn't current; it's expired. You are pulled over, then it's clear that the authority that was behind your ability to drive no longer exists. So, the issue really is who said that you are who you are? Who said you were a valid driver?

What's interesting is that God is silent at this inauspicious moment. It was God who at the baptism recorded in the preceding chapter made the great declaration, "This is my Son whom I love and with Him I am well pleased."[1] So, if that's the case, why is God silent now? Now, when the question is raised, where is the one who set this label in motion? Have you ever wondered, Black Boys and Men, where God was when someone was shining that light in your face? Have you ever asked yourself, "Where is God to back me up?" If not an angel helping out, it seems like at least something would happen to interrupt this interrogation. There is a hymn that says, *"Lord, I'm out here on your Word"*; that's all we have. The Word was all Jesus had when the devil was ready to do a smear campaign, mess with his mind, and wear him down.

I wonder why God does stuff like that. Do you ever wonder? Sometimes I do wonder, when I'm taking a stand for God and I'm doing so because I believe God has called me to take that stand, and I'm trying to be faithful, and I'm out there and I'm threatened and the light is shining, and I'm in a hostile environment, I've entered a danger zone, and I can't find any trace of God. I don't feel Him on the inside and don't see anything on the outside. The sun isn't shining, the birds aren't singing, and there's no wind whistling to remind me that God is the breath that keeps me alive in every moment. I have no clue that God is anywhere around and I'm just out there seemingly all by myself. Who's got my ear then; who is my attention on?

In Luke Chapter 2, it is recorded that Jesus and His family have gone on an annual pilgrimage and it suddenly occurs to Mary and Joseph that Jesus is missing. The fear of all parents is now their fear: where is he? Three days later, they find Him in the Temple sitting among those who should know this, that, and the other, and He's teaching. His mother said, "You worried me sick." Jesus said, "Why are you worried? Don't you understand I have to be about my Father's business?"

I recognize that when He said "my Father," we might believe that He understood who He was. But let me suggest that it's easy to believe we know who we are when there is a safety net beneath us, when we are still in our formative moments and there's a community around us to encourage us and to tell us what they see in us. It's one thing to be strong then, but when you're out there and there is no community and this divine affirmation has occurred and now heaven is silent, then what you gon' do? Who's got your ear then? To whom are you listening? Whose voice is in your head?

But, is it really possible to ever know who you are, what you're about if you're not asked? Is it really possible to know who you are and why you are? Is it possible to know that without somebody shining that light deep in the back of who you are to get a sense of what is there? How many times have you asked someone, "Tell me something about yourself," and they relay all the surface stuff, but after they are done telling you their name, where they went to school, and where they live, they have nothing else substantive to say. They sit there like a lump of clay with no purpose, no definition, and no direction. They are simply there waiting for someone else to fill in the blanks. It's easy to live by other folks' definition. But when they're not around, what are you going to do then? Who are you then? Who do you say you are then?

How could Jesus be about the Father's business if He were always in need of the Father reminding Him who He was? Let me suggest to you when the question "Where is God?" was raised, when the devil put an "if" in the face of Jesus, God was somewhere waiting for Jesus to believe that more than the son of Mary and Joseph, He really was from out of this world.

If that had not crystallized in his soul, He never would have survived the things that were on the other side of the moment. It is really a gift to you when someone really gets in your face and asks, Who are you? Who are you when your robe is off, when your nametag is off, when you go home? When you enter a room and nobody knows the real stuff about you, who are you then?

I was at a public event away from home walking along with a couple of other people when I heard a voice call out my name. When asked if I was going to answer, I said no. I kept walking because I did not know the voice. Away from home, away from the place of my formation, I would not turn around and investigate who was calling "Bernadette" because I did not recognize the voice. Who's got your ear? To whom are you listening and responding?

The film *The Butler* hit me so hard I was speechless afterwards. It took me a while to find my voice again. One of the things I was reminded of was the training for those who were going to engage in the boycotts. They were called some of everything in preparation so that they would not flinch when they were under fire. The day came when they went and sat at the luncheonette counter and folks got in their ear, called them the "N" word, told them they were nothing and poured ketchup on their heads, but they continued to sit there. Why? Because they had the right voice in their ear.

You can call me what you want, but I know who I am. I am a child of the Most High God, and wherever I am, I hear His voice calling me by my name and reminding me that I am His own. Who's got your ear? If God doesn't have your ear, you're going to be intimidated and you're going to be derailed. Other folk are waiting to fill in your blanks.

We are the people of God and as such, *we* speak and live like *we* know *whose* DNA *we* have! We know who we are and whose we are. We are a proud people. We are a capable people. We are a people with an amazing history. We are not only descendants of earthly kings and queens; we are children of the Most High King. Who's got your ear? I can hear the Savior calling…

NOTE

1. Luke 3:22, paraphrased.

Can You Taste It?

Violet Dease Lee

BIO. IN BRIEF

The Reverend Violet Dease Lee, Ph.D., was licensed and ordained to the gospel ministry of Jesus Christ by the Covenant Baptist Church in Washington, D.C., and served The Abyssinian Baptist Church for nearly 16 years. She is the first woman to serve as Assistant Pastor and the first to preside over the ordinances in Abyssinian's 205 years of Christian witness. Dr. Lee received the Doctor of Philosophy from Fordham University in 2012 and has been featured in *Glamour Magazine* as a top religious leader, *The African American Pulpit*, and *Upscale Magazine* as a top female in ministry within the Black Church.

Luke 9:23-27 (New Revised Standard Version)

Then he said to them all, "If any want to become my followers, let them deny themselves and take up their cross daily and follow me. For those who want to save their life will lose it, and those who lose their life for my sake will save it. What does it profit them if they gain the whole world, but lose or forfeit themselves? Those who are ashamed of me and of my words, of them the Son of Man will be ashamed when he comes in his glory and the glory of the Father and of the holy angels. But truly

I tell you, there are some standing here who will not taste death before they see the kingdom of God."

W e've all heard the sayings, "If you want something, you have to work hard for it." And, "No pain, no gain." And, "Anything worth having is worth working for."

If we think back to the beginning of the year, we might remember what we said we would accomplish. I'm sure some of us said we want a closer walk with God, and this passage of scripture will help us to accomplish that. If we keep doing the same things as last year, we'll keep experiencing the same results. It is not about resolutions but about right living.

This is one of my all-time favorite discipleship verses of scripture. Although found elsewhere in the synoptic Gospels, Luke's interpretation is the only one that attaches the word "daily." By doing so, the writer lets us know that this is an ongoing and never-ending process. Sometimes we need to be reminded that we are not altogether ready to meet our maker …that we are not saved and going to heaven in a hand basket …that we could never exhaust our efforts, our work for the Kingdom…that we must never give up. We are responsible for our discipleship every day! Just because you may have had a bad day yesterday does not mean that today will be the same. With each new day, we receive new mercies and compassion from God to help us make it through our daily tasks. Every job has specific responsibilities, but before you can perform them, you must undergo training. Discipleship is no different. It requires some training!

Our text today is not only apropos for us as we transition into new seasons of life, it is relevant any day and every day!

Once we've had an encounter with Jesus, we ought to ask ourselves, What does the experience mean? We should ask ourselves, What is the impact on my life? Who is the person Jesus and what does he really mean to me?

Today, we not only continue to celebrate the fact that God sent us a Savior, but we look to his life and teachings for our example. If last year wasn't your year, look to your Savior (as your example) and approach this year with greater hope and expectation. This is especially so when we encounter those moments where it seems that our lives are coming apart before our very eyes, when all that we have planned seems to disintegrate. When we don't even feel we can make it another day. We somehow don't remember that God is present with us every day and every step of the way. We don't remember that God is bidding us to come and give our burdens to the Lord. Sometimes we just need a little reminder, a push in the right direction and a plan that helps us re-think how this Christian walk can actually work.

For others of us, we need to know that this walk is doable. We need it to be demystified and made possible in a world that is so demanding, cruel, and sometimes cares less about our presence in it.

Well, I've come to tell you that all of this can be done. Jesus himself tells us the steps we must take, how important it all is, and the promises that will be fulfilled, if we would but obey him. The imperatives given seem quite demanding, somewhat radical, and maybe even a little harsh. Yet, they are possible. With God, all things are possible!

So what does Jesus require of disciples? There are three imperatives that we must follow: 1) Deny ourselves, 2) Take up our crosses, daily, and 3) Follow Jesus. Surprisingly, these instructions come *after* he has already *commissioned* the twelve, giving them power to go preach and heal everywhere. After he's raised the dead…after he's healed some sick folk! It comes after what is known as the Confession of Peter and on the heels of Jesus foretelling his imminent suffering and death. It also comes just before the transfiguration, when God acknowledges Jesus as the beloved one.

Don't you want to be called by God to do God's work in the world? Don't you want to know that you are God's beloved? Besides, what's the world's alternative? Why would you lose your life to a world that loves war more than peace? Why would you lose your life to a world that tears down our children, God's wonderful gifts to us all? Why would you lose your life to a world that is driven by economic gain and not love? Why would you lose your life to a world that devalues some people because they look or live differently, instead of embracing all of God's children in love? Why would you lose your life to a world that recognizes the wealthy and elite, but leaves all others to fend for themselves? Why would you lose your life to a world that doesn't value all of humanity enough to give them justice and equality? Why would you lose your life to a world that writes laws to tear you down and say you are inferior, because someone believes they are superior? Why would you, in the words of the great gospel songstress and preacher of the gospel, Shirley Caesar, "live in hell on earth, then die and go to hell"?

Now, what are the things in life that make us stop and say, "I want this so badly, I can taste it?" There are those aspirations in life that cause us to prepare a plan and work our plan until we reach our desired goal(s). At times, we find ourselves saying, "I want it so badly, I can taste it." You imagine that college degree and you say, "I want it so badly, I can taste it." You've already picked out the frame for the degree and you are only in your first year! The new job you want, "I want it so badly, I can taste it." You are already conjuring up new ideas and plans under your new position and title. But, you don't have the job, yet! You want to be an accountant so badly you can taste it. You want to be a teacher so badly you can taste it. You want to be a musician so badly you can taste it. You want to be a lawyer so badly you can taste it. You want to be a preacher so badly you can taste it! The new house you've imagined for you and your family... you've already been shopping for paint, window treatments, bathroom and kitchen fixtures, new bedding ensembles, and new furniture. Forget the fact that you haven't been approved for a loan yet! "I want it so badly and I can taste it." You may have been trying to conceive for years, to the point where you and partner will say, "We want a baby so badly, we can taste it!" You have drafted plans for the nursery and chosen the décor although you've never received a positive pregnancy test. These are some of the concrete things for which people pray, and want so badly, they can taste them.

What we don't walk around saying is, "I want to obey God so badly I can taste it!" We don't say, "I want to be a disciple of the Lord Jesus Christ so badly I can taste it!" Deacons, I don't hear people saying, "I want to study the word of God so badly I can taste it!" I don't hear people saying, "I want to see the kingdom of God so badly I can taste it!" I don't hear people saying, "I want to experience the kingdom of God so badly I can taste it!" What do you taste? Success? Wealth? A family? A deep desire to walk with the Lord and to do God's will?

Jesus comes to us and says, "If anyone would come after me, they must first deny themselves, take up their cross, daily, and follow me." First, we must deny ourselves those things that prevent us from drawing closer to God. Just as we try to deny ourselves that piece of carrot cake or that second helping of dinner, we must deny ourselves those things that keep us from becoming closer to Jesus. We must deny ourselves the opportunity to hit the snooze button on the alarm clock, repeatedly, morning after morning. That's when we need to get up and commune with God! We must deny ourselves that extra 20 minutes of sleep to incorporate a regular devotional period for the purpose of study, prayer, reflection, and praise. We must deny ourselves some music videos, TV shows, and texting time, and go to Bible study instead!

Next, we must pick up our crosses daily. When adversity strikes or we fall upon hard times, we must continue to hold tight to the cross of Jesus to guide us through the storm. Jesus lets us know that it is unacceptable to set aside your cross! You cannot declare that on Monday, Wednesday, and Friday—I will carry my cross. I will reserve Tuesday, Thursday, and Saturday for my days off. Then you'll say, "On the seventh day, God rested, so I'll take Sunday off, too!" Every time I recall this verse of scripture, I can see and hear my grandmother singing, "I've got my cross on my shoulder and I ain't gonna turn around!" Her defiant posture and her determined walk helped us to see that she made up her mind to serve the Lord, always!

Cross bearing is personal, but it is also communal. Do you bear the cross for others? Maybe you have a burden on your heart for our youth or men/women/children living with HIV/AIDS, or for helping children learn to read, or for young women and senior citizens with cancer. Maybe you care about homelessness or the mentally ill. In your time on earth, you will never awaken to a world that does not need your help.

You can't put your cross down because someone needs your voice and your help!

We're too quick to look for the easier method or the faster route. Everybody is looking for the hook-up or the pass thru! But Jesus requires that we work at building our discipleship. The Lord has made it clear that we must be intentional in order to follow Him. Thank goodness, Jesus is not saying what I used to see on cars so often. There was a popular bumper sticker that read, "Don't follow me. I'm lost." But Jesus is saying, "Follow me if you want peace that surpasses your understanding. Follow me if you want to know and live out your perfect purpose. Follow me, for I am the way, the truth, and the life." If you are lost, follow Jesus.

I don't know about you, but if Jesus is telling me that I may experience a little bit of God's kingdom while I'm on the earth before He returns, before experiencing death, then I want some of that. I want to taste it! You see, the slave masters used to tell our ancestors that they had to wait until the other side to get their reward. But when we learned to read "the good book" for ourselves, we found Jesus saying, You don't have to wait to experience the kingdom!

What would a glimpse of the kingdom look like? No poverty and discrimination in Ethiopia, no AIDS in sub-Saharan Africa, no fighting among Israelis and Palestinians, no threat of nuclear war, no war in Afghanistan, no terrorism, no starving children in America or anywhere in the world, no racism, no sexism. No ageism or other "isms" that separate us. No homelessness. No disease. No suicide. No overcrowded prisons…and nobody left behind. That's right…from Compton to Cairo and from Hampton to Holland no one would be left behind! Just more Jesus joy and the best for others!

Jesus wants to teach you how to love, how to increase your joy. Jesus offers you salvation or restores the joy of your salvation because the joy of the Lord is your strength! I can taste it, because every day with Jesus is sweeter than the day before!

Can you imagine a taste of the kingdom being like that of homemade biscuits, Mama's fried chicken, even grandma's baked pies, whether apple, peach, or sweet potato—they were all mouth-watering delicious! Elders may have led me to the faith, but I had to accept Jesus for myself. Oh yes, I had to taste and see that the Lord is good! He's been my joy when I felt down! He put a smile on my face when I was starting to frown! He picked me up and turned me around; placed my feet on solid ground! The Lord's been better to me than I've been to myself!

I've tasted His JOY!

I've tasted His PEACE!

I've tasted His FORGIVENESS!

I've tasted His PROTECTION!

I've tasted His MERCY!

I've tasted His LOVE!

What about you? What about you? What about you?

An Attitude of Gratitude

Joanne J. Noel

BIO. IN BRIEF

Reverend Dr. Joanne J. Noel's purpose is to serve God
by using her gifts, skills, and academic knowledge to challenge,
inspire, equip, and empower her students to reach their
highest and fullest potential. She is an Associate Professor
of English at Pillar College in New Jersey. She is an ordained
Baptist clergywoman, a columnist, and an editor, and
she is currently working on a second doctorate in the
humanities at Union Institute & University.

Luke 17:11-19 (New International Version)

*Now on his way to Jerusalem, Jesus traveled along the border between
Samaria and Galilee. As he was going into a village, ten men who had
leprosy met him. They stood at a distance and called out in a loud voice,
"Jesus, Master, have pity on us!"*

*When he saw them, he said, "Go, show yourselves to the priests."
And as they went, they were cleansed.*

*One of them, when he saw he was healed, came back, praising God
in a loud voice. He threw himself at Jesus' feet and thanked him—and
he was a Samaritan.*

Jesus asked, "Were not all ten cleansed? Where are the other nine?
Has no one returned to give praise to God except this foreigner?" Then
he said to him, "Rise and go; your faith has made you well."

Y ou can't be grateful if you are not thankful, and you
can't be thankful unless you are grateful. Thankfulness
proceeds from gratefulness and gratefulness precedes
thankfulness.

Gratefulness is not taking for granted what you have been
given because of God's favor, which is a manifestation of God's
grace and goodness.

In order to have an attitude of gratitude, we must first
recognize what has happened. Recognize where you were
and from where God has brought you.

The text says, "And one of them when he **saw** he was
healed…" Now the lepers didn't ask precisely for healing but
for pity. That could mean anything: "Help us out with some
money, clothing, food, or healing…" Jesus was a King but he
didn't have silver or gold, so he gave them the best he had.
He was setting them up for a miracle. "Go show yourselves to
the priests…" Only a priest could declare a person healed of
leprosy. And as they went, they were cleansed.

It is not quite certain what biblical leprosy was. Although
some may associate it with "Hansen's Disease," it could also
be any number of diseases of the skin. It was infectious and
incurable. Leprosy in biblical times was an alienating disease.
According to the Levitical Code, the person with this disease
must wear torn clothes, let his hair be unkempt, cover the
lower part of his face, and cry out, "Unclean! Unclean!" Imagine
that. It's not bad enough that you have an incurable, infectious
disease; you have to tell everyone who does not have it, "Stay

away from me because if you just touch me, I could kill you."
You have to announce your own pain. You have to announce
your own tragedy. Everyone else gets to hope no one else finds
out about the worst secret in their life, but you have to shout
yours from the roof top. As long as a leper has the infection, he
remains unclean. He must live alone or in a colony with other
lepers; he must live outside the camp."[1] Leprosy also made a
person ritually unclean. To touch a leper defiled a Jew almost as
much as touching a dead person.

One thing is certain, this leper **recognized** that something
had happened to his skin. In his going-in-obedience he was
cleansed. The narrator, Luke, who is also a physician, doesn't
tell us how he recognized he was healed, but something about
him had been changed and he knew it. Like the old church
deacons used to say, "Well, I looked at my hands, my hands
looked new; I looked at my feet and they did too." I think that's
what this leper did.

And once he recognized the miracle, he **returned**. He came
back. In reading and reflecting on this narrative, I began to think
of some of the places and spaces to which I need to return in
order to give back as an act of thankfulness. And there are some
of you who also need to return to those places and spaces from
which God has rescued you, healed you, and cleansed you in
order to serve and to give back as an act of thankfulness. Some
teacher saved you when everyone else had you believing that
you were only worthy of the academic trash heap. You need to
return to that school or some school as an act of thankfulness.
Some recreation center saved you from the streets, prison, and
an early death. You need to return to that center or some center
and help some kid who is traveling down a dead-end street.
Some neighbor, who was not a relative, looked out for you, fed

you, and just helped take care of you. You need to return to that neighbor and bless them, or bless some senior who now needs someone to look out for them, make sure they're fed and taken care of. We all have some places to which we need to return as an act of thankfulness.

The returning leper was a Samaritan; often it is not the people we expect to return to give thanks who do it. It may not be the alumni who has become famous and wealthy. It may not be the people in whom we have invested our time, money, and talent. It may not be the person who received everything the Church had to offer. But one thing's for certain, it will be someone who was cleansed from something, recognized it, and returned.

When we are not grateful, it says either that we despise what has been given or done for us or we don't consider it consequential enough to warrant our thanks. Or, we can become so consumed with what has been done that it blinds us from seeing that the ONE who has blessed us is worthy of praise. In other words, we appreciate the gift more than the giver. We don't have the good sense to recognize what has happened and return to give thanks. Is there anything worse than an ungrateful person? Is there anything worse than the person you give a gift who gives you a blank stare and a barely-got-it-out thank you? Is there anything worse than a child who expects to get gifts and takes them for granted; they believe that the world owes them something? Is there anything worse than a spouse who does not appreciate a home-cooked meal, a clean house, and well-behaved children? They are under the delusion that their spouse is just supposed to make it happen all the time. Is there anything worse than an ungrateful person?

I think several of those postures apply to the lepers, especially the last one. They appreciated the gift more than the giver. Jesus' instructions were, "Go and show yourself to the priests…and as they went, they were cleansed…" Only one leper had sense enough to recognize that it was not the priests who were the source of his healing, but Jesus, and so he returned **rejoicing**. He had an attitude of gratitude.

Rejoicing is the act of giving thanks for favor bestowed. Of course, as New Testament believers, we ought to thank God daily just for who God is: merciful, compassionate, patient, exuding lovingkindness, clothed in splendor, robed in greatness, majestically glorious, forgiving and giving. Our thankfulness is based on our recognition that God is God, supreme, sovereign, holy, GOD.

But, when God has done something for us, we ought to **give thanks, too**. The lepers had stood at a distance and called out in a loud voice, "Jesus, Master, have pity on us!" But how many of them recognized they were cleansed, returned, rejoiced, and gave thanks? God is and will always be greatly concerned about our needs. However, after being blessed, instead of an attitude of gratitude, some of us treat God like a 'ginormous,' celestial vending machine. We put in a prayer and expect to receive a prize. Some of us take a spiritual bucket list approach to the Deity. God has answered this prayer or that concern, and so we can scratch it off our list.

There is a sense of entitlement within the fiber of American Christianity. We are certain that God owes Americans something. Too many Americans act as if they are due responsive government, even if they do not vote or refuse to put bad candidates out of office. Too many Americans act as if they are due great neighborhoods, even if they raise hellish children and do not participate in the upkeep of where they live. Too many Americans act as if they are owed wealth, even if they made their money due to bad tax laws and the labor of the poor.

One missionary to China recently shared with me how Chinese Christians had to worship YHWH in secrecy. However, some of us take our freedoms and blessings for granted. Some of us are at ease in Zion because we have conformed to culture and wrapped the Gospel in a neat little package with a bow and labeled it "prosperity Gospel." So instead of an attitude of gratitude, we have developed an attitude of "Name it and claim it," "Call it and haul it," or "Blab it and grab it." I wonder if this is not some form of spiritual leprosy.

As a preacher, I must confess that I need to put in more prayers of thankfulness. I need to throw myself at the master's feet in thankfulness more often. But some preachers are not thankful just for the fact that God is using us. They are more focused on popularity and prestige; instead of being faithful, they want to be famous. Instead of being powerful spiritually, they want to be power brokers. They want mega churches and mega ministries to feed their mega-egos.

Some parishioners are not thankful that the Gospel is being preached; they have itching ears. If it's not the speaker we like, if it's not the pastor or Bishop, we tune out. If it's not the topic we want to hear preached, we harden our hearts. Spiritual leprosy takes many forms, but an attitude of gratitude brings us to worshipful thanksgiving. An attitude of gratitude brings us to worshipful thanksgiving even if our favorite choir is not singing and the preacher has an off day. An attitude of gratitude brings us to worshipful thanksgiving when no one else is around. We can worship and thank the Lord anywhere, in our car or in our bedroom. Anyone know what I'm talking about? You start thinking about how good God has been to you, and before you know it, your soul cries out, hallelujah, thank you, Jesus!

The ten lepers had cried out loudly in unison, "Have pity/mercy/compassion on us!"

Now here we have this one leper, a foreigner rejoicing for what has been done for him. He is praising God in a loud voice. Whereas he had remained at a distance, now he comes close in worshipful thanks and "threw himself at Jesus' feet and thanked him—and he was a Samaritan."

The Samaritans are allegedly descendants of Ephraim, Manasseh, and Levi, who are despised by 'full-blooded' Jews because they were considered half-breeds—a mixture of Jews and the peoples who were brought to inhabit the Northern Kingdom after Israel was taken captive and into exile by Assyria in 722 BCE. They claim Abraham as their forefather but assert a different place/location for worship, Mount Gerizim, as opposed to Jerusalem.[2]

However, this despised Samaritan didn't feel entitled and perhaps that's why he **recognized**, **returned**, and **rejoiced** in what had been done. Neither did he ask for the next thing. His heart was full with thankfulness, which manifested in loud praises. He felt obligated to give thanks. He had an attitude of gratitude.

What the text suggests is that the people who don't feel a sense of entitlement are those who often recognize the magnitude of the blessing and feel most obligated to give thanks.

But God is so good. Look at this. God will bless you some more if you thank God for something God has already done!

What kind of God is that! It's a mighty good God. It's a God who is better to us than we are to ourselves. It's a God who is good to us in spite of us.

Jesus asked, "Were not all ten cleansed? Where are the other nine? Has no one returned to give praise to God except this foreigner?" Then he said to him, "Rise and go; your faith has made you well." For having an attitude of gratitude, this man received what Matthew Henry calls "a spiritual blessing" too. I know we want physical blessings, especially if we are sick and need healing, and I don't know about you, but I want "a spiritual blessing" too. I want more faith. I want more joy. I want more peace. I want more of the Holy Ghost. I want to forgive more. I want to walk right. I want to talk right. I want to love everybody in my heart. I want "a spiritual blessing" too.

With an attitude of gratitude we recognize what God has done; we return (go back to God and acknowledge the great things God has done or go serve people in the places from which we were delivered); and we rejoice, and give God thanks for just being God and for blessing us too.

NOTES

1. Leviticus 13:45-46.

2. Information adapted from http://www.jewishencyclopedia.com/articles/13059-samaritans.

It Is Finished

Angela Anderle

BIO. IN BRIEF

Reverend Angela Anderle is a member of Trinity United Church of Christ in Chicago, Illinois, and serves its Prison Ministry preaching in state and federal correctional facilities. Angela received her Masters of Divinity from North Park Theological Seminary. She is the creator and producer of the internet radio show *Revelation: The Gospel According to House*. On the program, she uses house music and the gospel to address spiritual, social justice, and other needs of listeners in over 57 countries. *Revelation* ministers to listeners daily on gospelaccordingtohouse.podomatic.com. In 2014, as co-owner of *Above the Vibe* radio (ATV), Rev. Anderle will seek to provide a new platform for artists and community leaders to radically transform and bring people together from around the world.

John 19:26-30 (New Revised Standard Version of the Bible)
When Jesus saw his mother and the disciple whom he loved standing beside her, he said to his mother, "Woman, here is your son." Then he said to the disciple, "Here is your mother." And from that hour the disciple took her into his own home. After this, when Jesus knew that

all was now finished, he said (in order to fulfill the scripture), "I am thirsty." A jar full of sour wine was standing there. So they put a sponge full of the wine on a branch of hyssop and held it to his mouth. When Jesus had received the wine, he said, "It is finished." Then he bowed his head and gave up his spirit.

When parents hold their newborn for the first time—as they count their toes, trace the lines that resemble Mama's nose on a tiny face, hear the first cries break forth from a mouth that holds daddy's smile—in those early moments when the breath of new life first fill the lungs, what parent believes that their baby will live life as an outlaw?

What parent believes that their infant child will one day be executed as an enemy of the state? What parent believes that they will have to leave their homeland to hide their infant to keep him or her from being killed? Surely not Mary and Joseph. After all, the presence of their oldest baby boy was announced to them personally by angels. They had been visited by an entourage of wise men from the east who brought expensive gifts. Plus, shepherds told them that God's glory lit up the entire night sky as if it were day when their child was born.

On top of that, Mary and Joseph had already been through enough dealing with their families since Mary got pregnant during her engagement. Joseph hung in there with his pregnant bride-to-be whom he hadn't had relations with despite his doubts and the gossip that raged around the neighborhood. Then they gave birth alone, away from their families, among animals in a barn. Surely, with all of this, great things were ahead for this child. They had to be. Didn't they?

Yet shortly after the men from the east left, an angel appeared to Joseph in a dream and said, "Get up, take the child and his mother, and flee to Egypt, and remain there until I tell you, for King Herod is about to search for the child and destroy him." Joseph then took his family and fled by night and went to Egypt.

The government, led by King Herod, labeled Jesus an outlaw from birth. Those who didn't know the real reason why may have thought that label was affixed because of his home town of Nazareth. The town was so pitiful, people would ask, "Can anything good come out of Nazareth?" the way they now ask, "Can any good thing come out of Chicago, Detroit, or Africa's Congo?"

The outlaw label really stuck because Jesus started doing Kingdom preaching. This put him further at odds with the king. What king wants to hear an outlaw talk about his own kingdom? On top of that, Jesus provoked the king by saying things like, "Go tell that fox (meaning King Herod) for me, I am casting out demons and performing cures today and tomorrow, and on the third day I will finish my work."[1] Jesus was not looking for a fight, but he wasn't running away from one either. He intended to do what he came to do.

Labeled as an outlaw, Jesus still accomplished his work. He still included the excluded, healed the un-healable, forgave the un-forgiven, lifted the lowliest, and discipled the undisciplined. He still taught the temple teachers, turned the theology of the religious leaders upside down, mowed down outdated cultural mores, stood up for sisters, and left his legacy in the hands of a group of flawed followers.

He accomplished his work! Then the day of reckoning came. There is a price to be paid for turning the world upside down. The temple police put out an APB (all-points bulletin). Attention, all camel units: Be on the lookout for a most wanted suspect. Description: His hair looks like wool, his eyes like flames, his feet like bronze, and his voice is as the sound of rushing waters. We've set up a sting. He will be identified by one of his followers, who is now a confidential informant for us. The informant's name is Judas. When Judas kisses the suspect, that's our sign to move in for the arrest. But, proceed with caution, for some of his followers are known to carry knives. Consider them armed and dangerous.

Jesus is taken in by force like an outlaw. He is denied, abandoned by his closest disciples, and sentenced to die like a common criminal. Jesus, who names himself "The Resurrection"; Jesus, the one who calls himself "the way, the truth, and the life"—is on his way to be crushed on a cross.

Among his final words from the cross, Jesus says, "It is finished." But, as the work of Jesus, Emmanuel—God with us—in human flesh, found its victorious completion from the cross to an empty tomb, all was not finished. In fact, this was a new beginning!

For Jesus, ending his life on a cross is not to have failed or finished. When he says, "It is finished," he does not mean I am done. He does not mean all work is completed. For Jesus, "It is finished" means part one is done, part two will be done by my followers, and I will finish it all when I return. For Jesus "it is finished" means something new can begin.

So what is beginning? He was beginning a new work in his followers then and now. This new work requires the Holy Spirit which Jesus breathed on his disciples. It requires believing that Jesus is the Son of God, so that we may have life in his name. And it requires that his sheep be fed.

Jesus begins in us the work of holding fast to our partnership with him as the hope that anchors our soul. Holding fast so that endurance has its full effect, so that we may be mature and complete, lacking in nothing. Holding fast like Mary and Joseph, who enduring shame and abandonment, pushed ahead when a community made no room for them.

Jesus began in us phase two. He completed phase one; it's finished. Now it's our turn. Jesus delivered us from the bond of eternal damnation—that's finished, and he began in us the work of deliverance of those who are bound by society and circumstances. Do you know anyone who is bound? In your household, your neighborhood, your city? Of course you do. Well, Jesus has begun in you unbinding work. So, go preach, teach, baptize, and unbind some folk. Go pray, rally, march, and unbind some folk. Teach, feed, uplift, and unbind some folk. Build something, tear down something, resurrect something, and unbind some folk. Stop something, start something, **do something**, and unbind some folk!

Those of us who follow Jesus are on the hook. He left us a legacy, lessons, and the life-giving power of the Spirit to continue his unbinding work. Someone said, "It is not what we preach or say but what we **practice** and **believe** that makes us followers of Christ." Martin Luther, said, "A religion that gives nothing, costs nothing, and suffers nothing, is worth nothing."[2] What's your religion worth? Nathan Schaeffer said, "At the close of life, the question will not be, 'How much have you gotten?' but 'How much have you given?' Not 'How much have you won?' but 'How much have you done?' Not 'How much have you saved?' but 'How much have you sacrificed?' It will be 'How much have you loved and served,' not 'How much were you honored?'"[3]

But not only has Jesus begun in us unbinding work, he has also begun in us binding work. Most of us understand unbinding work and a few of us are even willing to do it sometimes.

But when it comes to binding work, that's a different matter altogether. We're not up for that. That's the preacher's job. That's the work of activists. That's a bit much; it doesn't take all of that, we tell ourselves. But Jesus did call us to binding work too. He chased the moneychangers out of the temple. That's serious binding work. What moneychangers have we chased out of our community lately? Those selling reverse mortgages that end up putting seniors out of their homes, payday loans that can charge up to 300% in interest, or title loans that deprive people of their cars and charge steep interest need to be bound. Our folk are the first to be bound. So let the binding of those who rob our people be one of our first priorities.

Probably the biggest agent we need to bind is the Prison Industrial Complex. The Prison Industrial complex has its hands around the necks of more of our men and women than slavery did a decade before the Civil War began.[4] As Reverend Martha Simmons said at Duke University, "Prisons are NOT first and foremost a means of reducing crime or a deterrent to crime. If they were, we would not have such high incarceration rates and relatively the same crime rates throughout MOST of history. Prison systems are mainly about power and money and their maintenance. They count on the fear, life fatigue, and ignorance of the general public to allow them to keep devouring generations without much public out-cry or backlash, even from the Church…To change the prison problem in the US, we first need to understand that change will not occur because of one big revolution, but due to a continuous stream of small changes in one consistent direction—the direction of divine justice. The civil rights movement was not one big revolution; it began the day slaves on their way to the shores of the Americas jumped overboard rather than be enslaved, and the struggle continues today even 50 years after Martin spoke of his dream."[5]

We need to stop disavowing and limiting our binding power. We can do more about these hard problems than we are doing. I heard the story of a seminary professor who drove into the school parking lot. Before getting out, he snapped "the club" onto his steering wheel, stepped out, locked his doors, and then activated his alarm system. A student saw what happened and said, "Professor, don't you believe in the power of God (the sovereignty of God) to protect your vehicle?" The seminary professor replied, "You know, I teach about the sovereignty of God. But I also believe in the total depravity of man to destroy it." Stop giving the devil so much credit.

This makes too many of us gawkers, just watching each crash go by. We watch seniors deciding between eating and buying medicine, and we just say a prayer and go home. We watch all the people starving around the world, and we just change the channel and go on about our business. We watch all of the sad headlines from the news, but we don't take any action when we hear about what needs to be fixed. We just sit on the sidelines and gawk in despair. Get off the sidelines and get in the fight. Do some binding work.

Finally, you should know that if you do Jesus work, it will succeed because of the authority he has given to us. It is the authority of Jesus from the cross that begins and succeeds in our work as we turn the world upside down. It is finished, so we have the authority to reconcile the world to God through the Good News. It is finished, so we have the authority to fix the schools that mis-educate and under-educate our children. It is finished, so we have the authority to expose the deceptiveness of drug addiction, and shut down the cash registers of the Prison Industrial Complex.

We who by the victory of Jesus the Christ beginning in us have done the work of loving and administering justice; we who by the victory of Jesus beginning in us have done the work of quenching the raging fires of all forms of oppression; we shall not fail, because our Savior said, *It is finished.*

By the victory of Jesus on the cross, Jesus says to us it is finished—I begin in you victory—you, the light of the world. Jesus tells us, It is finished—I begin in you victory. "I have said this to you, so that in me you may have peace. In the world, you will face persecution. But take courage; I have already overcome the world!"[6] Jesus tells us, it is finished—I begin in you victory, "for the one who is in you is greater than the one who is in the world,"[7] "for whatever is born of God conquers the world."[8]

This is the moment of our life—Jesus says, It is finished— I begin in you. This is the moment of our lives; this is the day! Jesus commands, It is finished—I begin in you—and Jesus confirms it, It is finished. It is finished—I begin in you—this day and every tomorrow. And no eye has seen nor ear heard, nor human heart conceived, what God has prepared for those who love him. It is finished—I begin in you.

NOTES

1. Luke 13:32, NRSV.
2. Martin Luther quote online at http://www.truthsource.net/quotes/?q_sort=authors_list&sort_author=Martin_Luther.
3. Nathan Schaeffer quote online at http://www.searchquotes.com/quotation/At_the_close_of_life_the_question_will_be_not_how_much_have_you_got,_but_how_much_have_you_given%3B_no/32278/.

4. Michelle Alexander, *The New Jim Crow: Mass Incarceration in the Age of Colorblindness* (NewYork, NY: The New Press, 2nd edition, 2012).

5. Sermon by Martha Simmons delivered at Duke University, Gardner C. Taylor Lectures, 2013, online at http://divinity.duke.edu/initiatives-centers/black-church-studies/gct.

6. John 16:33, NRSV.

7. 1 John 4:4, paraphrased.

8. 1 John 5:4, paraphrased.

Hosea and the Cost of Pride

Tytrea Baker

BIO. IN BRIEF

Reverend Tytrea Baker was called to ministry at Apostolic Church of God under Bishop Arthur M. Brazier. She is an ordained Associate Minister at Apostolic Church of God in Chicago, Illinois. She graduated from North Park Theological Seminary in Chicago with a Masters of Christian Ministry and was certified as a Spiritual Director by North Park Theological Seminary. She taught in the Santa Clarita Christian Center, which is a part of Kenneth Copeland Ministries, and has served as a prayer leader and intercessor for several national gospel artists.

Hosea 5:5-7, 15 (King James Version)

And the pride of Israel doth testify to his face: therefore shall Israel and Ephraim fall in their iniquity: Judah also shall fall with them.

They shall go with their flocks and with their herds to seek the LORD; but they shall not find him; he hath withdrawn himself from them.

They have dealt treacherously against the LORD: for they have begotten strange children: now shall a month devour them with their portions.

I will go and return to my place, till they acknowledge their offence, and seek my face: in their affliction they will seek me early.

In Leviticus 21, the role and lifestyle of High Priests are clearly outlined. Some of us as Saints have become High Priests in our own mind. We think **more highly** of ourselves than we ought, rather than thinking of ourselves with sober judgment, in accordance with the measure of faith God has given us.[1] This is due to an out-of-control spirit of pride. The spirit of pride will consume you, obscure your vision, and lead you to destruction. We don't realize how pride has ruled us when we get to a certain place on our jobs, in church, and especially in government. We begin to believe the hype and our own press releases. We forget that all of gifts, talents, and abilities were given to us **for God's glory, not our own**. Remember that—it directly applies to the story of Hosea.

The name Hosea means salvation. Hosea was a "Minor Prophet," which only means that his text and message were brief in comparison to Major Prophets such as Isaiah. This refers not to the importance of their prophecies, just to the brevity of their prophecies.

Little is known of his history; it is presumed that Hosea was from the Northern Kingdom of Israel because of the vast knowledge of this region shown in his writing. That would mean that he was from the same region as Jonah.

It is ironic that both of these prophets were given a task that was outside the norm of the Jewish tradition. How many know that God still sometimes takes us out of our faith tradition to do a new work in Christ Jesus!

Hosea was given the task of marrying a harlot, thereby symbolically taking on the sins of Israel. Jonah was given the task of bringing a warning of repentance to the people in the city of Nineveh, and these were people who had harmed Jonah's people. How many of us have become angry when God gives a second chance to someone we believe deserves to be punished? We want grace and mercy for ourselves but not for our enemies.

Both prophets experienced jarring assignments to their lives and hearts, and their work affected a nation. Hosea had to live in what could be called a desecrated marriage. Jonah's task was to bring salvation to a city that appeared to be worse than Sodom and Gomorrah.

Hosea prophesized while under the rule of King Jeroboam II in Israel. The nation had peace and prosperity alongside corruption and spiritual bankruptcy. Hosea's contemporaries were Micah and Isaiah, who also prophesized in Judah in the southern Kingdom.

The underlying construct for the book of Hosea is God's loyalty to us while we are in the midst of our rebellion and idolatry toward Him. I will briefly explore the book of Hosea and the concept of pride using three themes. These three themes are foresight, insight, and hindsight.

Chapters one through three of Hosea describe an adulterous wife and a faithful husband to show us the concept of **foresight**. Foresight is the ability to predict or the action of predicting what will happen in the future. Hosea was informed by God about his marriage to Gomer and what it would entail and the spiritual ramifications. However, Hosea did not foresee how this marriage would affect his heart and mind. Hosea and Gomer's understanding of their marriage demonstrated their flawed foresight. However, their marriage clearly demonstrates the flawless foresight of God. Symbolically the marriage was needed to demonstrate the harlotry of Israel. But it was also to illustrate that God wanted Israel to discover the love He had for them, just as Hosea would discover his love for his unfaithful wife, Gomer.

God still has this relationship with the flawed people of God today. God is still sending prophets to tell us that we are loved and that we continue to be unfaithful to God. Ultimately, because God knows us so well, God had the **foresight** to know that we would need a Savior. For without a Savior, given our pride, we would all be lost in our continuous sin and continuous unfaithfulness to God. Jesus is God's clearest illustration that God loves us. Our rejection of Jesus, and the Word, make clear that pride can overwhelm us and cost us eternally.

Insight is the understanding of a specific cause and effect in a specific context. Insight is shown in the naming of Hosea's three children: Jezreel, which means in Hebrew "God will sow"; Lo-Ruhamah, which means "not having obtained mercy"; and Lo-Ammi, which means "for ye are not my people and I will not be your God." This naming of Hosea's children showed insight into the heart and mind of God concerning Israel. God knew that their pride would keep derailing their blessings and that they would reap what they had sown. They would not obtain mercy, and God would disown them because they disowned God.

Chapters four through fourteen give us further insight into adulterous Israel and our faithful Lord. Adulterous Israel is found guilty in chapters four through six. Just as Israel is found guilty of adultery, so is Hosea's wife, Gomer. However, Hosea is commanded to stay with her as God stays with adulterous Israel. Adulterous Israel is put away in chapters six through ten, but not forever. This is not the end of Israel.

Hindsight is the ability to understand after something has happened what should have been done or what caused the event. Beginning with our text in chapter five and continuing in chapters seven, ten, and eleven, it is shown that if Israel had not been blinded by pride, and had obeyed God, they would have been spared captivity. How many know in hindsight that if we had obeyed God, we would have been spared captivity from those things that plague our lives?

In chapter eleven and part of chapter thirteen, the destruction of Israel is discussed in graphic terms. Hosea 13:9 says, "You are destroyed, O Israel, because you are against me, against your helper." Here the scripture speaks to the people being destroyed for lack of knowledge. They have no hindsight, foresight, or insight. They, like Gomer, did not see the error of their ways. No matter what God does, their pride will not let them repent and turn to God instead of away from God.

Saints, we too have this problem. How many times have we been led astray because of a lack of knowledge? Webster's Dictionary says knowledge is "the fact or condition of knowing something with familiarity gained through experience or association, condition of being aware of." The word knowledge is mentioned 130 times in the King James Version of the Bible. This signifies how powerful and necessary knowledge is to a child of God.

But, how many times were we warned and given knowledge, and because of pride decided not to heed the warning? Or if the information was before us, we did not access it. When this happens, knowledge becomes like a light switch that was not turned on. Or we heard the word and rejected it because it did not come in the form or package or voice we could or would receive. Pride will make you foolish! It will keep you from going after the information you need to live for God and for your best interest.

How many times have we refused to learn something because of our pride? Woulda', coulda', and shoulda' begin to whip us when we look back in hindsight.

Because God cares for us, even when we are prideful, God in compassion gives us a remedy, just as he did Israel. He tells them in chapter thirteen that He will "reclaim and redeem" them. Yes, they will suffer for their sins; God will have justice. But, because God is also the justifier, God, not us, can decide who gets His forgiveness. Thanks be to our compassionate God that when pride blinds us and takes away our foresight, insight, and leaves us with hindsight evidence of the mess we made, God still wants to reclaim and redeem us.

I pray this over this congregation: That we will become accountable to one another and to God. Father, help us accept responsibility for our actions as we gain wisdom and knowledge from You. Let us not stay prideful, thereby costing us valuable time with You. Show us the more perfect way. Lead and guide us into all truth so that we will become more profitable to you and the kingdom and edify the body of Christ! Let us live so that your name is highly lifted, given all the honor and glory, and all the praise. In the matchless name of Jesus! Amen.

NOTE

1. Romans 12:3, KJV.

OTHER PUBLICATIONS BY MMGI BOOKS

These Sisters Can Say It! Volume 1
Edited by Cynthia L. Hale and Darryl D. Sims

Motivational Moments for Women
By Joanne Noel and Darryl D. Sims

Motivational Moments for Preachers
By Charles E. Booth and Darryl D. Sims

Motivational Moments for Men
By George W. Farmer and Darryl D. Sims

Navigating Pastoral Leadership in the Transition Zone
By D. Darrell Griffin

*Standing on Holy Common Ground:
An Africentric Ministry Approach
to Prophetic Community Engagement*
By Lester A. McCorn

Evangelizing and Empowering the Black Male
Edited by Darryl D. Sims

*Adam Come Home:
Liberating the Minds of Black Men*
By Darryl D. Sims

Order your copies today!

Online at mmgibooks.com
and at Amazon.com

For discounts on bulk orders,
please call 773.314.7060.

L